Management And Performance

A STUDY OF THE EFFECTIVE FUNCTIONING OF LIBRARIES

Management and Performance

A STUDY ON THE EFFECTIVE FUNCTIONING OF LIBRARIES

KARUNA SAHA

GIAN PUBLISHING HOUSE
NEW DELHI - 110002

GIAN PUBLISHING HOUSE
4-C, Ansari Road, Daryaganj
New Delhi-110002

ISBN—81—212—0389—9

PRINTED IN INDIA

Published by Mrs. Gayatri Garg for Gian Publishing House,
New Delhi 110002.
Printed at Godwall Printers, Delhi

DEDICATED
TO
THE MEMORY OF MY PARENTS

Preface

Modern life is dominated by large, complex and formal organisations of various kinds with diverse aims and varying size. Many of these organisations are created with specific social objectives and large public funds flow into them by way of Government investments. In India, during the VIIth plan, an outlay of Rs. 6,383 crores was made for the development and maintenance of educational organisations like schools, colleges and universities. It is essential for the economic, social and cultural growth of a nation that these organisations function effectively and play their role in the development of various sectors of society. The libraries are one such complex formal organisations which aim at providing support to formal education and research as well as impart informal education to their users.

Besides the economic input in terms of resources, the functioning of an organisation is influenced by the interaction between individual and organisation. The organisational design, climate and management styles, influence the performance of the individual whose behaviour at work in itself is influenced by several other psychological factors. How to find out the attributes of excellent performance of an organisation becomes an important issue ? After having studied one hundred companies in U.S.A., Thomas and Waterman (1982) in their book on 'In Search of Excellence' have arrived at a few important attributes of excellent performance, the prepondrance of which was observed in good companies identified by them. Some of the attributes discovered were : bias for action, closeness to customers, autonomy and enterprise, and simple form and lean staff.

As a practising librarian and researcher of organisational behaviour, it was my endeavour to discover the facts that influence the functioning of libraries and the attributes that may be applied to measure their effectiveness. The present book is primarily based on my research work for Ph. D. In this work, the 'user's satisfaction' or 'closeness to customers' as agreed upon by Thomas and Waterman also, was taken as one of the attributes of library effectiveness. Viewing libraries as growing organisms, the 'growth index' was taken as the second factor and 'employee's job satisfaction' as the third one. Even though in most of the research studies job satisfaction is taken as a measure of individual performance, the choice of this factor as a measure at effectiveness of organnisations was based on the recent researches on organisational behaviour by Porter et al. (1975) who emphatically advocated that the satisfaction of personal goals and social needs of the employees is one of the major objectives of the modern organisations. Finally, keeping in view the 'Team Work' requirements of libraries, the group performance Index, instead of individual performance, was taken as the fourth attribute of effective library performance.

Having identified the parameters of good performance of libraries, the study had been designed to discover whether the effective function which was being measured by the four attributes described above, would be influenced by the size of the organisation i.e. large, medium and small ; task structure indicating allocation of work, placement and training and the background of the employees ; structural factors as reflected in the division of labour, degree of specialisation, and supervisory staff-ratios ; policies of reward, punishment and training ; communication and decision-making patterns and the degree of inter-unit coordination.

The other area of investigation was whether any differences existed in the functioning of special and academic libraries ? If yes, which were the factors responsible for these differences ?

Attempt had also been made to study whether a clear cut distinction would emerge between the least effective and the most effective libraries on the basis of attributes of performance. If yes, whether the factors accounting for significant differences in their functioning can be identified ? The answers to these queries were found in the results obtained which are being discussed in this book. The data collected from the users had also been separately analysed to study if their satisfaction was influenced by any of their background factors like age, sex, educational and professional qualifications etc., in addition to identifying important library dimensions influencing their satisfaction. The results of this study make interesting reading and are discussed at great length in the book.

The data had been collected from 203 employees, 200 users, 30 supervisors through questionnaires and interviews and from the organisational records of fifteen special and academic libraries in Delhi. The libraries surveyed were Delhi School of Economics, Delhi University Science and Law libraries; South Delhi Campus library, All India Institute of Medical Sciences and National Medical libraries, National Science library, Indian Law Institute library, Jawaharlal Nehru University library, Libraries of Institute of Defence Studies and Analysis, Archaeological Survey of India and Indian Council of World Affairs libraries, Indian National Science Academy library, Nehru Memorial Museum and library and The Indian Institute of Technology, Delhi library. The data had been processed carrying out factor analysis, computing standard deviations, coefficient of correlations and mean differences.

The book is presented in 10 chapters. Chapter I presents the introduction and discusses the concept of management and performance. Chapter 2 enumerates the concept of organistional effectiveness as viewed by different authors, its relevance to non-profit organisations and an overview of literature incorporating both empirical and theoretical studies conducted in India and abroad. Chapter 3 explains effectiveness in library organisations and presents both the Indian and Foreign studies. Chapter 4 deals with the theoretical framework, different models and approaches to effectiveness and the design of the study. Chapter 5 discusses the factors chosen as the measures and correlates of effectiveness. The rationale for choosing the factors and their proposed relationship to the field of investigation have been discussed in detail on the basis of which a set of hypotheses are developed. Chapter 6 explains the instruments—the questionnaires and other tools used in data collection. Chapter 7 discusses the methodology—the sampling techniques, size of the sample and methods of data collection, processing and analysis. It explains in detail how the objective and subjective data obtained through different tools and from varied sources was reduced to a compatiable organisational level to conduct this macro study. Chapter 8 presents the results and discussion of the study. Chapter 9 brings out the prominent findings and presents a summary and Chapter 10 makes important observations and suggestions.

My thanks in preparing this work go to Shri Mohinder Singh the Librarian and my other colleagues at the I.I.T., Delhi library for the help and encouragement given by them. I am thankful to my other colleagues in library profession who have painstakingly helped me in data collection and at other stages of investigation. Shri A.L. Kapoor, Shri M.R. Moonga and Shri B.S. Adhikari (Delhi School of Economics), Shri Satish Chander and Shri G.A. Shastri (Delhi University Law and Science libraries, Shri H.C. Jain (South Delhi Campus library), Shri B.D. Ukhal (National Science library), Shri and Shrimati Suba Rao (Institute of Defence Studies and Analysis and Archaeological Survey of India), Mrs. K. Verma and Shri S.K. Bhatnagar (Nehru Memorial Museum and library), Shri Jamedkar (Indian Council of World Affairs), Shri Ramaswamy and Shri Sube Singh (National Scienee library), Shri Debral and Garg (National Medical library) require special mention for their generous and kind help extended to me during the investigation.

I remain greatly thankful to the Director, I.I.T. Delhi for permitting me to undertake the research work on which this book is primarily based and to my supervisors Prof. P. Mathur and Dr. Anuradha Sharma of the Department of Humanities and Social Sciences, for their guidance and support during the course of study. Special thanks are due to Prof. J. Kurian

(Louisiana State University, U.S.A.), who while at the I.I.T. Delhi helped me at every stage of data processing and Prof. B.R. Handa of Department of Mathematics who greatly assisted me in the interpretation of the results. This work could not been completed but for the spontaneous support, inspiration and cooperation received from my husband Shri P.K. Saha and children Biplab and Aparajita for which I shall ever remain thankful to them.

Even though the necessity to familiarise with the techniques and principles of management is knocking at the doors of library managers and professionals, many of us feel shy of entering into an arena hitherto considered to be an exclusive domain of management experts. I sincerely hope that book will create sufficient curiosity and interest in the minds of library professionals to make them ask for further managerial inputs.

During the course of research, I could hardly lay my hands on any comprehensive book on organisational performance encompassing different interpretations, models, theories, approaches and components. The field remain vast and varied, leaving students, teachers, and managers in a perplexed state. It is my earnest hope that teachers, researchers and practioners of organisational behaviour in general and library professional in particular would find this book stimulating and a valuable guide.

Library
I.I.T., New Delhi

KARUNA SAHA

Contents

Page No.

List of Tables

List of Appendixes

List of Figures

1

Introduction

Management as a distinct field to study has emerged out of long experience acquired in business and industry. The large economic and human inputs needed in manufacturing and selling the products necessitated special knowledge and skills in handling these activities over the years. This empirical knowledge with contributions from other disciplines like mathematics, psychology, statistics and economic has been organised to form a distinct discipline known as management science. 'Management' is being defined as a process or activity that brings together man, resources and technology to accomplish set organisational goals. Accordingly, organisation, individuals, resources, technology and organisational goals become important components of the management science.

The management activity involves the planning, organising, motivating and controlling of the man, material and resources in a way that organisational goals are accomplished within a given time frame. In other words, it requires that organisations perform effectively. A set of principles of scientific management has been given by the thinkers and experts of management science to provide practical guidelines in managing organisations of various kinds including industries, schools, colleges and libraries. The libraries are important social institutions and require large funds to establish and maintain them. It is essential that they function effectively fulfilling the roles assigned to them. For achieving efficiency and effectiveness in functioning, it is also imperative that they are organised on the basis of principles of scientific management.

The four important principles of management given by classical thinkers are : (a) Unity of command, (b) Equal authority and equal responsibility (c) Delegation of authority, (d) Limited span of control. The first principle stipulates that to have the best performance from an employee, he should be made answerable to one superior only. The second principle demands that if an individual is made responsible for a task, he should have full authority to take necessary action for its execution. The third principle enumerates that there should be judicious distribution of work and decentralisation of authority and the fourth stipulates that a manageable number of employees be made responsible to a superior so that he can control them efficiently. New dimensions are being added to the principles of management enunciated by the classical thinkers. To make the classical model dynamic, feed back to the employees and from the employees to the manager has been incorporated in the management concept. But even this was not enough.

After the famous Howthrone studies at Western Electric Plant in U.S.A. in 1924, Elton Mayo emphasised the human element in management. His studies showed that when working conditions like shorter working hours, company lunches, scheduled rest period and cohesive grouping were introduced, the efficiency of the workers increased. Later when these benefits were removed the productivity did not decline. It was discovered that the concern of the management for the worker in the form of facilities given led to the feeling of affiliation and achievement. Satisfaction of personal needs and improvised interpersonal relations were the positive factors affecting productivity. Constant research is going on to understand the employee's psychology at job and the concept like jobs enlargement, job involvement and job characteristics are being studied by the behavioural scientists to help the manager in designing the jobs that would lead to positive outcome at work places. Does he possess the requisite qualification and skill ? Does he feel involved in the job ? Does he enjoy autonomy at work ? These are some of the important questions that the managers should address to themselives while designing jobs for their employees.

Recent researches have also shown that the managers that encourage participation of their subordinates in decision-making and provide them with more identity and autonomy, contribute to organisational effectiveness by making feel more responsible. The other areas drawing the manager's attention for effective organisational performance are : the organisational design, reward and punishment, distribution policies like performance appraisal, promotion and training, organisational climate, inter-unit coordination and effective management styles. It is being argued that to be effective, the managers of nineties should think emphatically and cross-culturally, they should learn to balance the needs of organisation with that of the individuals and be ready to give away authority rather than grabbing it.

To run an organisation, the manager or the leader of an organisation has to perform certain functions. The management functions generally performed by a leader are : (a) Planning, (b) Organising, (c) Motivating, (d) Controlling. Planning involves setting up programmes, projects and activities to be undertaken over a period of time. For an example, in a library set up planning may involve a programme to introduce computerisation and setting targets for switching over from manual operations to mechanical ones in a phased manner, or planning a new building or its extension, anticipating the quantum of demand for equipment at a future date or setting up targets for a new information dissemination service.

Once the targets are set, the organising activities set in. This will involve providing for man, material and resources for the project conceived. While aiming at introducing computerisation, a library would need to procure hardware, develop or acquire software, and train or select staff to undertake different jobs. The librarian has to strive and approach the higher authorities to have equipment, resources and personnal needed to carry on the project.

Along with planning and organising, manager has to play a part in influencing the level of performance of the employees. In other words, motivate them to contribute their best. William James of Harvard university, in his research on motivation had discovered that hourly employees in U.S.A. could save their jobs only by working approximately 20 to 30 per cent of their ability, whereas if highly motivated, they were capable of working upto 80 to 90 per cent of their ability. The performance level of employees becomes low, if motivation is low, even though apparently it may be taken as if the employees have lower ability. If properly motivated, this untapped area of employee's ability becomes a big potential of human resources and can lead to tremendous increase in productivity. Since motivation provides access to vast human potential it would be interesting to discuss it in little more detail here.

Motives are the needs, drives or impulses within the individuals that are the driving forces behind human activity or behaviour. Of the competing motives, the motives that are not strong are given up and the motives that are satisfied do not prove to be driving force. According to Abraham Maslow (1954) there seems to be a hierarchy into which human needs arrange themselves. Maslow classifies the needs as : (a) Physiological, (b) Safety (c) Social, (d) Esteem and (e) Self-actualisation.

Physiologicals need for food, clothing and shelter tend to have the highest strength until they are some what satisfied. Once physiological needs are satisfied, need for security and safety become dominant. The employees concern at this stage would be whether he is able to retain his job and provide food and shelter to his family for tomorrow. Once he is confirmed in his job and is able to meet physiological and safety needs, the social and esteem needs assume importance. The employee passing through this stage would expect more respect and recognition. However, at times, the employees may not always seek recognition through mature and adaptive behaviour but through irresponsible actions. The management has to find out avenues to canalise his energy in proper direction through discussion and dialogue. The self-actualisation is the desire to attain what a person thinks he is capable of and is the ultimate goal of his career or life.

In the achievement of needs or goals it is not essential that all the individuals systematically go through different stages and also strive for the ultimate. Different individuals may have different hierarchial preferences and may feel satisfied at any one or the other level. Yet, it is amply proved by many studies conducted in behavioural science, that in modern society where physiological needs for food, shelter and clothing and safety are satisfied by secured job conditions, the monetary reward in terms of salary no longer act as motivating factor for the employee to perform at the maximum level. The manager has to take note of this fact and has to create on environment in which employee's social, esteem and self-actualisation needs are satisfied within the work set up. The fair policies of reward and punishment reflected in genuine performance appraisals, promotions and training, pursued by the manager would definitely provide positive motivation to the employees.

Once targets are set, resources are provided and individuals are motivated, the manager has to perform the controlling functions involving feed back of results and follow-up to compare accomplishment with the plans, making necessary alterations and changes in the execution of projects necessitated on the basis of feed beck. The management functions, described and discussed so far, are inter-related and at any one time, one or more become of primary importance. Later on a few more functions were added to the list of management functions which are aptly described by the term POSDCORB given by Luther Gulik. The functions enumerated by this term are: planning, organising, staffing, directing, coordin a reporting and budgeting.

To perform management functions, the manager may require different kind of skills which may be described as : (a) technical, (b) human relation and (c) conceptual skills. Technical skills require knowledge of the rules, methods and techniques, and ability to apply them in performing specific jobs. These are acquired through education, training and experience. For an example, to manage technical work in a library, the skills needed would be the knowledge of the rules of the classification and catalouging, different methods of indexing, and familiarity with computer languages and their applications. The manager needs to possess another kind of skills called human relations skills. He should have a good flair for handling human relations as his role involves working through individuals and groups at different levels.

The manager may be handling people at pear level, subordinate level or at senior level. Different kinds of human relation skills would be needed to work through individuals at different levels. To be a skilful manager of human relations, the librarian should have proper feed-back from different sources, be aware of his perception by his staff and should involve them in proper dialogue to sort out difficult and sometimes conflicting interests of his seniors, colleagues and subordinates.

The manager or the librarian would also require conceptual skills to understand the complexities and functioning of the overall organisation and to act according to the objectives of the total organisation rather than according to the immediate needs of a group or set of users. Faced with demand by a group of users for certain facilities like special information service, he has to perceive its impact on demand from other corners, the manpower or other resources available at his disposal and the other objectives he has set to accomplish, before he attempts to meet such a demand.

The appropriate proportion of the skills required by a manager varies as he advances from supervisory positions to top management position. As we may observe, at the supervisory level of an Assistant Librarianship, more of technical skills and less of conceptual skills are needed. The Assistant Librarian is required to train and develop other employees, and supervise technical work, whereas he does not have to plan and function in an over all perspective. The chief librarian, however, may not require more of technical skills as these jobs are carried out by his junior colleagues, but he should possess a clear over all perspective of the organisation to plan and execute in broader organisational as context in addition to being an expert in handling human relations. The librarian at the middle level management should possess technical, conceptual and a fair degree of human relation skills. The management of human relation is crucial to librarians or managers at all the levels, as all of them will be performing tasks through individuals and groups and a good knowledge of their behavioural and motivational patterns is necessary for influencing the employees to work efficiently.

Another important aspect of organisational study is goal setting. Unless organisations set goals, how can their performance be judged ? Setting up the values humanises the organisations and forms the basis of organisational culture. It may not be known to many Senior Executives of a modern successful organisation like IBM, which set the objectives of their organisation as early as 1914. The foremost among their goals were that individuals must be respected, excellent and superior performance must be pursued and customers must be given the best possible service. The organisations may set broad objectives which are perceived as their culture as well as specific goals and targets for each of its component divisions.

Having discussed the principles of scientific management, management functions, skills and goal setting, we address ourselves to the question of effective organisational performance. Effectiveness has assumed greater importance today, in view of large inputs of manpower and resources needed to run the organisations. The organisations differ in size, complexity and characteristics. There are business organisations whose performance can be measured in terms of sales and profits. There are informal organisations like family and churches and formal service oriented organisations like schools, hospitals and libraries, whose performance cannot be defined or measured in terms of profit or sales. At the same time the economic inputs that enter into their making and their capacity to influence social and cultural aspects of life, urge upon a practitioner or researcher in organisational behaviour to define and identify the parameters of their effective functioning. By identifying the indicators of effective functioning of service organisations, we would be providing a great tool in the hands of planners, administrator and executives, be which to judge the utility or wastefulness of public funds flowing into these organisations and to take remedial steps to reappropriate them in right channels.

2

Organisational Effectiveness : Concept and Review of Literature

Organisations, today are thought to be the most rational form of social groupings created to fulfil a great variety of social and personal needs (Etzioni, 1964). A large number of authors have devoted their attention to the study of the organisations, their behaviour and efficient functioning.

Bernard (1938) defines on organisation as :

> "A system of consciously coordinated activities of forces of two or more persons" (p. 37).

Weber (1947) defines an organisation as :

> "A system of continuous purposive activity of a specified kind" (p. 15).

By thus defining an organisation, Bernard (1938) stresses the role of individuals who must communicate and take conscious decision towards a common purpose. Weber (1947), on the other hand, views an organisation as a system of purpose oriented activities.

Etzioni (1964) adds further dimensions to the existing definitions of organisations when he states :

> "Organisations are social units (or human groupings) deliberately constructed and reconstructed to seek specific goals . . . " (p. 3).

Etzioni also highlights other important dimensions of an organisation such as, its structure as seen in division of labour and authority distribution, the process of communication, decision-making and performance appraisal. All of these are directed towards the achievement of goals of the organisation.

Argyris (1964) defines organisations as :

> "Open systems imbeded in, but constantly influencing and being influenced by the environment" (p. 12).

Katz and Kahn (1966) look at organisations as systems engaged in maximisation of return and further introduce the concept of interaction between organisation and its environment.

Steers (1977) defines organisations as :

> " . . . Complex entities that strive for rational allocation of their resources for purposes of goal attainment" (p. 2).

Kast and Rosenzweic (1981) look at the concept in the following way :

> "Organisation implies structuring and integrating activities, that is people working or cooperating together in interdependent relationship. The notion of inter-relatedness suggests a social system" (p. 6).

The review of definitions suggests that from a system of consciously coordinated activities or forces of two or more persons (Bernard, 1938), organisations have become complex entities (Steers, 1977) and psycho-social systems (Kast and Rosenzweic, 1981). Their functioning is characterised by closer relationship among structured activities which are always attuned to goal attainment. The very objectives of organisations imply their effectiveness. The degree to which the organisations are successful in accomplishing their objectives will obviously depend on how the human and material resources are coordinated to achieve the objectives.

Organisational Effectiveness

Organisational effectiveness, defined in very general terms, is the degree to which a system or an organisation accomplishes its objectives. The systems or organisation may have multiple objectives which may vary from organisation to organisation. These multiple objectives, at times, may be contradictory. The studies of effectiveness are concerned with how well these objectives are defined and achieved, and the factors that influence the process of goal achievement.

An effective organisation should have clearly defined goals, well designed organisational and task structure, employee oriented policies and a free and open channel of communication in order to secure dependable performance from its employees and to offer them a good deal of satisfaction from their roles. An organisation has to be viewed in its totality.

Effectiveness thus covers the entire gamut of organisational activity : defining goals, design of structure, distribution of work, productivity, placement of employees and formulation of procedures, coordination, policies of reward and punishment, performance appraisal and training, leadership style, decision-making, methods of communication and the behaviour of the employees. Edgar H. Schein (1976) expresses the same view in the following statement :

> " . . . It would be a mistake to assume that if one selected the right people and trained them to do the job, effectiveness would be insured. It would be equally erroneous to assume that the establishment of mutually satisfactory psychological contract with employees, or the reduction of inter-group competition or leadership training, any of

these alone would guarantee effectiveness. Rather, the systems conception leads us to a different way of thinking about the problem . . . " (p. 119).

Bennis (1962) views effectiveness as follows :

> "If we have to view organisations as adaptive, problem-solving organic structures, then inferences about effectiveness have to be made, not from the static measure of output, though these may be helpful, but on the basis of processes through which the organisation approaches problems" (p. 273).

Bennis lays emphasis on internal processes through which the organisation achieves its output etc.

Argyris (1964) defines an "organisation as an effective one if it attains its core activities : (a) achieving its objectives (b) maintaining itself internally (c) adapting to its external environment".

Katz and Kahn (1966) define organisational effectiveness from different frames of reference. Defining it from the organisational frame, they state organisational effectiveness as :

> " . . . Maximisation of returns to the organisation by all means" (p. 170).

Explaining it from individual's frame of reference, they state the following :

> "We can discuss organisational effectiveness from the point of view individual member, defining as the most effective that organisation which offers the greatest aggregate returns to the member" (p. 166).

Apart from organisational and individual frames of reference, they also take into account the super-system, the society, of which the organisation is a part :

> "At this level, the effectiveness of the organisation would be assessed in terms of its contribution to the efficiency, survival power and environmental control of the entire societal system" (p. 166).

Beckhard (1969) describes a healthy organisation as one that is aware of, open to, and reactive to change. He believes that such organisations search for new forms and methods of organisation, entrust employees with more responsibilities that are satisfying, confront conflicts rather than avoid them, and try to ensure open and free communication.

Steers (1977) defines organisational effectiveness as :

> "... Organisation's capacity to acquire and utilize its scarce and valued resources as expeditiously as possible in pursuit of its operative and operational goals" (p. 5).

Chung and Megginson (1981) define organisational effectiveness as :

> "An organisation's ability to realise its multiple goals (such as profit, stability and so forth) and its ability to adapt and survive in a changing environment (through adaptability, environmental control, survival, and so forth)" (p. 506).

Thus, it becomes clear that the concept of organisational effectiveness has been defined and interpreted from several angles by different authors. Its interpretation ranges from the maximisation of returns to the organisation, to the maximisation of returns to the individual member (Katz and Kahn, 1966), from the attainment of feasible goals (Steers, 1977), to the capacity of the organisation to maintain itself internally and adapt itself externally (Argyris, 1964). Attempts to define this concept has led social scientists to study its processes (Bennis, 1962) or characteristics of survival, growth, and environmental control (Katz and Kahn, 1966). Further, different criteria have been used to study the concept of effectiveness.

Effectiveness in Non-profit Service Organisations

Discussing the effectiveness of non-profit making service organisations, Evans (1983) states that no concrete indicator of effectiveness, such as profit, is available for judging service organisations. Effectiveness, here, may involve a value judgement of what is appropriate for each organisation.

Cameron (1980) has specifically outlined the characteristics of such organisations encompassing school, colleges, and large service institutions that make their assessment a difficult task. The important characteristics outlined by him are the following :

Characteristics of Servicc Organisations

Ill Defined Goals

In service organisations, goals are generally ill defined, complex, changing, and at times contradictory. The sub-units may be pursuing goals that may be unrelated to the broader organisational goals.

Unclear Means-End Relationship

No obvious connection between the technology (the way work is done) and the outcome exists in such organisations. It may be difficult to identify a successful outcome, let alone, finding the agreed-upon means to perform the task.

Little to no Feedback from the Output to the Input or from the Input to the Output

The information exchange between the recipients of service and the producer of service is quite poor or non-existent. The connection between the input and the output are not testable.

Weak Linkages between the Sub-units

In service organisations, there exist a few common structures or linkages that can bind the sub-units together. The most common linkages of the technology, goals or pattern of authority are either not present or are very weak.

Widely Differing Criteria of Success

In such organisations widely differing criteria of success may be operating simultaneously in different parts. Pursuit of success in one part may inhibit success in the other parts of the organisation.

Libraries, as service organisations, display characteristics similar to non-profit organisations and face similar problems in their evaluation. Cameron (1980) expresses the view that for such organisations there cannot be a perfect evaluation, but effectiveness can be improved, if some critical issues in measuring organisational effectiveness are clearly sorted out. He is of the opinion that a study for evaluating service organisations can be designed carefully by keeping in mind the vital issues pertaining to such organisations. Once these issues have been examined critically, different data and criteria can be selected for the purpose of evaluation.

A study of the literature will reveal further the criteria, correlating factors and approaches that have been recognised as significant in studying the effectiveness of profit-making organisations and other service organisations such as libraries.

Studies on Effectiveness

Both theoretical and empirical work have been done in the field of organisational effectiveness. Some of the Studies are discussed below which show how the concept of effectiveness has been viewed and operationalised.

Theoretical

Bennis (1962) views organisations as adaptive and problem-solving organic structures and maintains that inferences about effectiveness have to be made on the basis of process through which the organisation approaches its problems. He further states that deductions about effectiveness have to be related to the efficiency of the processes. He maintains that single measure of profit or output achievement cannot be a measure of organisational effectiveness.

Argyris (1964) views effectiveness of an organisation in term of achievement of its core activities, such as (1) achieving objectives, (2) maintaining the internal system, and (3) adapting to external environment. These core activities should be achieved with a decreasing or constant input, while maintaining or increasing the output of the system. Argyris emphasises the systems approach to the concept and states that inter-relatedness among the elements of the system should be focused.

Blake and Mouton (1964) state that an organisation is effective, if its managers exhibit a high concern for people and work. When the managerial concern for both people and production are high, there is high productivity, high morale, and creativity, through team action. The individuals are engag-in de goal-oriented interdependent efforts, and therefore, the organisation is effective.

Katz and Kahn (1966) describe organisational effectiveness within two frames of reference. One is the organisation itself as a system in its own right, and the other as part of the larger society or system of which it is a sub-system. They define organisational effectiveness as the maximisation of returns to the organisation by economic, technical and political means. This is measured by the success with which it obtains the inputs it requires on advantageous terms. This is from the organisational frame of reference. From the frame of reference of the supersystem, effectiveness would be assessed in terms of the organisation's contribution to the efficiency, survival power and environmental control of the entire societal system. The organisation would be effective if it provides maximal return to the society for the energic demands it makes on society.

Yutchman and Seashore (1967) have used various models in studying the area of effectiveness. Their strategy was to start with a large number of variables describing the performance of the organisation and then to examine the pattern of relationship among them in order to find out the underlying dimensions of performance from this pattern. Under the system resource model, they define effectiveness in terms of the organisation's ability to secure an advantageous position in its environment and to capitalise on that position to acquire valued resources.

Price (1968) based on a review of fifty studies of small business firms, prepared an inventory of propositions to measure effectiveness. He recognised the existence of five systems within an organisation such as economic, population, ecological, internal and external political systems, and untrue systems. The organisational behaviour is judged in terms of response of these systems. The responses are in terms of productivity, adaptiveness, institutionalisation, confirmity and morale.

Porter et al. (1975) hold that organisational behaviour is determined by the characteristics of the individual and the organisation. The individual when he enters the organisation brings with him his own skills and needs and the organisation has its own expectations (from the individual) and the resources to offer to the individual. The individual adjusts his work behaviour according to his perception of organisational rewards. According to Porter et al., the overall effectiveness of the organisation may depend upon making a poor or good fit between the organisation and the individual.

Steers (1977) studies the concept in terms of attainment of operational or operative goals. He states that the greater the progress that is made towards such goals, the more effective is the organisation. He evaluates the concept under a process model and identifies four major seats of variables that influence organisational effectiveness. These are the following :

1. Organisational characteristics
2. Environmental characteristics
3. Employee characteristics
4. Managerial policies and practices

Steers concern remains with goals that are feasible and can be operationalised.

Campbell (1977) adopts goal approach in assessing the organisational effectiveness. He is rather concerned with the questions of what goals, criteria and standards should be chosen to assess the effectiveness of the organisation.

Cummings (1983) views the concept of organisational effectiveness from the point of its constituents and the extent to which they perceive organisation as capable of meeting their demand. He, in fact, builds upon Porter et al's views wherein organisations expectation and resource and individual's need and skills jointly determine the behaviour in organisation. The organisational variables (like leadership, task design) are studied in terms of their impact on the participants who look upon the organisation as an instrument of achievement of their valued ends. From this perspective he perceives :

> "An effective organisation as one in which the greatest percentage of participants perceive themselves free to use organisation and its sub-systems as instrument for their own end" (p. 197).

Pearce and David (1983), based on a review of the literature in the field, have offered a design-performance and a set of hypotheses to serve as guides to empirical researches. They believe that previous researches have failed to establish a relationship between organisational design and performance. The reason why they believe so is that organisational level characteristics first affect the group structural properties which in turn have an impact on performance.

Veldsman (1984) has tried to integrate different approaches (like goal, system resource, and process), different units of analysis and strategies into one combination making it a cube. The evaluators can then indicate their position on each dimension of the cube and study the concept accordingly.

Empirical

One of the first attempts to study effectiveness by multivariate approach was made by Georgopoulos and Tennenbanum (1957). They argued that organisational effectiveness should be studied by using systems theory rather than viewing it from one angle only. They defined effectiveness as the extent to which an organisation, as a social system, given the resources and means, fulfils its objectives.

Looking at organisational effectiveness from the point of view of its goals, Georgopoulos and Tennenbanum argued that the definitions of organisational success must consider not only the objectives of the organisation, but also the means through which objectives are achieved. They conducted a study on 32 industrial service units. The effectiveness of the organisations were measured in terms of productivity, absence of intergroup conflict, flexibility. The data were obtained through a questionnaire. The result indicated that the above criteria can be used as a measure of organisational effectiveness.

Burns and Stalker (1961) argued that the most effective design of the organisation is determined by the environmental factors. They surveyed twenty British electronics firms to establish a relation between the environmental characteristics and managerial practices. They identified the organic and mechanistic styles of management depending upon the degree of environmental stability. The mechanistic systems were characterised by condition of control and authority, extreme task specialisation, and vertical line of communication. The organic systems had horizontal line of communication, decentralized authority. They then related each style of management to organisational effectiveness depending upon its environment. For example, in an automobile industry where market and technology remain the same over longer period, mechanistic style would result in effectiveness, whereas in an aerospace industry were environments are always changing, organic management style would result in effectiveness.

Friedlander and Pickle (1968) studied effectiveness in terms of the need satisfaction of the system components. The major components were the internal systems like the owner and the employee and societal components like the customers, suppliers, creditors, community and the government. The satisfaction of different components was measured by different inventories. The result of the study indicated moderate relationship between the need satisfaction of the owner and employee and other societal components. Even among societal components, concurrent fulfilment of need was rather low. They recommended that an organisation, in order to be effective, should strive to achieve higher satisfaction of its different components.

Mott (1972) has defined and elaborated the concept of organisational effectiveness as the ability of an organisation to mobilize its centers of power for action, production and adaptation. He conducted studies on a variety of organisations and came to the conclusion that effective organisations were characterised by higher production rates besides symbolic adaptability and flexibility. The factors influencing the effectiveness were found to be the clarity of objectives, rules, policies and guide-lines, functional integration, and a rational trust environment. Mott thus argued that organisations can be differentiated by means of perceptual criteria, such as, quality and quantity of products, efficiency, adaptability and flexibility etc. Based on these, he suggested eight point scale of effectiveness.

Khandwalla (1973) examined the relationship between

organisational design and profitability of 79 firms. Organisational design variables consisted of : (a) uncertainty reduction variables measured by staff support and vertical integration ; (b) differentiation variables measured by degree of decentralisation of authority, divisionalisation; and (c) integration variables measured by level of sophistication, participation and control in management. Profitability was measured by average pre-tax profitability over the past five years. The finding of the study on the basis of grouping of the firms into high and low profitability groups was that highly profitable firms exhibited a higher co-variance among the organisational design variables than the marginal firms.

Child (1974) conducted a study on more than 80 British service companies and about 800 managers working in them were covered. The growth index for the companies consisted of their percentage growth in income, sales turn over and net assets. This was taken as an indicator of performance. The factors influencing performance were taken as : (a) managerial attributes like the age of the manager, (b) organisational attributes like objectives of the organisation, ownership and control, size of the company, allocation of resources for different functions, environment and technology. The findings of the research, however, did not establish a very strong relationship between managerial and organisational variables and company's performance. The explanation given in Boswell's view is that 'if a vast number of influences on performance are at work, then no single factor is likely to have much effect of its own.'

Osburn and Hunt (1974) carried out a study that focussed on environmental complexity as it relates to effectiveness. The sample selected were service organisations. The environmental complexity is viewed in terms of three interrelated variables : (1) risk in the environment—organisation relation (2) dependence of organisation on environment for growth and survival ; (3) the nature of inter-organisational interaction (favourableness, or unfavourableness). The correlation of these variables effectiveness was then studied. The questionnaire method was used to collect data. The result indicated : (a) Risk variable unrelated to effectiveness, (b) Environmental dependency and inter-organisational interaction were positively and significantly related to effectiveness, (c) The most closely related variable to organisational effectiveness was inter-organisational interaction.

Knowles (1975) conducted a study in fourteen organisations to find out the relationship or interdependence among ten dependent and independent variables. The variables chosen were production, quality, cost, labour turnover, job satisfaction of operations, job satisfaction of supervisors, work anxiety, industrial unrest etc. The respondents were asked to rank the variables. Individual ranking measure showed wide and consistent variations among sections, within sections variables were found to be consistently inter-related. The organisations were divided into two groups on the basis of performance. The high performance organisations were characterised by favourable attitude, achievement, and organisational stability. The other group was characterised by considerable dissatisfaction and organisational instability.

Gilsson and Martin (1979) examined the effectiveness of human service organisations. Thirty organisations rendering different human service (drug abuse, family counselling, welfare, mental health) participated in the study. Four hundred and eight workers filled the questionnaire measuring the organisational variables. The variables measuring effectiveness were productivity and efficiency. The main findings were (a) centralisation positively related to productivity and efficiency, (b) formalisation has a marginal negative relation with productivity and efficiency, (c) formalisation is positively associated with centralisation. Though this research appears to explain the productivity in service organisations, the links between the organisational variables and productivity are not well drawn. Only two major organisational variables i.e. formalisation and centralisation are taken, all other variables are left out. The functional relationship between the measures of effectiveness was also not clearly defined.

Van de Ven and Ferry (1980) reported the findings of their longitudinal studies conducted in State Government Security offices in the United States. The data for the study were collected from organisational records as well as through various sets of instruments. The organisations were assessed at three different levels : Macro (organisational), Micro (individual), and unit level. Different sets of instruments were used for different levels of assessment.

The effectiveness of the organisation was measured in terms of efficiency, effectiveness, and job satisfaction of the employee. Final analysis was done by studying the correlations of independent factors and measures of effectiveness. The result of the studies showed substantial correlations between structural and other factors and measures of effectiveness such as job satisfaction, efficiency and effectiveness. The authors, however, clarify that different sets of results may be found in different types of organisations even with the same instruments.

Weiner and Mahoney (1981) conducted a random study of 193 manufacturing corporations. The data were collected from various types of reports. Measures of corporate performance were profit, profitability and stock prices. The factor influencing these were assumed to be organisation, environment, leadership. The variables chosen under these were industrial sales, industrial competition (environmental) ; size and technology (organisational), capital structure and capital strategy (leadership). Regression analysis was used to arrive at the result. The result indicated that stock prices display relation with all dependent variables. The profitability was shown as function of organisational and leadership variables. These two variables were shown to play significant role in organisational effectiveness.

Cameron (1981) conducted a study on 41 colleges and universities in seven states in North-Eastern United States. The nine dimensions of effectiveness chosen were : student-education satisfaction, student academic development, student career development, faculty and administration employment satisfaction, professional development and quality of faculty, system openness and community interaction, ability to acquire resources and organisational health. The variables influencing effectiveness of these organisations were presumed to be : (a) organisational variables as structure and environment, strategic emphasis of administrators, organisational goals ; (b) financial variables; and (c) demographic context variables.

Discriminant analysis was used to predict differences in domains of effectiveness among different groups of institutions. Different types of institutional groups identified were : (a) scholarly-high morale group ; (b) scholarly-medium morale group ; (c) externally oriented group, and (d) medicore group. Significant differences were observed among four groups of institutions in their domains of effectiveness.

Cameron (1983) in a longitudinal study analysed the causal relationship between organisational effectiveness of colleges and universities and faculty unionism. The specific interest was to find out whether ineffectiveness leads to unionism, or whether unionisation leads to ineffectiveness. Since the purpose was to find out causality pattern, cross-legged correlation analysis was used. The effectiveness of the institution was measured by nine dimensions already used by Cameron (1981). The questionnaires were administered at three different times i.e. 1976, 1980, 1983. Mean scores were computed for each of the institutions on each of the nine dimensions of (OE) and an overall mean score was also determined. The results indicated that in each of the three years, unionised institution scored lower than non-unionised institutions on the effectiveness dimensions. The result also indicated preponderance of causality between ineffectiveness leading to unionism over the years. Effectiveness in unionised institution does not improve over time.

Peters and Waterman (1982) based on their empirical study of excellent firms in U.S.A. have identified eight main factors that were found in excellent firms. These factors were (i) bias for action, (ii) closeness to the customers. (iii) autonomy and enterprise, (iv) productivity through people by treating rank and file as the root source of quality and productivity, (v) hands on, value driven i.e. being achievement oriented, (vi) stick to knitting, never acquiring a business that cannot be run and (vii) simple form lean staff (viii) simultaneous loose-tight properties. Though not all the factors were present in all the companies, yet a preponderance of eight was visible in good companies.

Goldsmith and Clutterbuck (1985) have also identified main

factors constituting excellence in successful firms in U.K. The factors identified were : leadership, autonomy, control, commitment in the management level, close interaction with the market, zero basing, innovation factors, and integrity perception.

Studies Conducted in India

While surveying Indian literature on organisational effectiveness, one can lay hands on a large number of studies on organisational structure and processes, a few on organisational climate, change, and environment and a very few directly on organisational effectiveness. Some of the studies dealing with organisational climate, change and environmental aspects which have implications for organisational effectiveness and have been conducted in India are given in Table 2.1.

TABLE 2.1

Indian Studies on Climate, Change and Environment

Researcher	Title of the Study
1. Robock (1962)	Management in Underdeveloped Countries
2. Sequeria (1964)	Organisational Climate in Indian Industry
3. Pareek and Lynton (1965)	Sensitivity for Personnel Organisational Development
4. Sharan (1968)	Climate of an Organisation
5. Bajaj (1981)	Alienation as Related to Perception of Organisational Climate
6. Lal (1932)	Organisation Climate in Academic Libraries in India : A Pilot Survey
7. Ansari & Rub (1982)	Executive Success as a Function of Leadership Style—Organisational Climate Fit

Studies on Effectiveness

Sengupta (1969) conducted a study in electric lamp manufacturing firm in West Bengal. The study was based on the interviews of the staff members. The result of the study indicated that factors like specialisation of function, learning of business through practice and short-term profit orientation were some of the causes of malfunctioning of the firm. The author emphasised the need for human organisation to improve the functioning of the firm.

Negandhi and Reimann (1973) conducted a study in 30 manufacturing units in India. The measures of effectiveness consisted of behavioural and economic indices. Under behavioural Index, manpower acquisition, employee satisfaction, manpower retention, interpersonal relations, interdepartmental relations, and manpower utilization were included. Under Economic Index, growth in sales, net profit were covered. The result of the study indicated that decentralised organisations were more effective in behavioural and economic terms. These organisations were also characterised by fewer layers of hierarchy and a participative style of decision-making.

Agrawal (1975) conducted a study in two hospitals to compare the performance of a good hospital with that of a problem hospital. Stratified random sampling was done to select the respondents from among the staff to elicit their opinions on organisational health. The different components of organisational health taken were : organisational goals, personal goals, job satisfaction, coordination, and inter-group relations, superior-subordinate relations, intra-organisational strains, organisational adaptation. The performance of the hospitals was judged in terms of satisfaction of the patients. The result of the study indicated significant mean differences in the satisfaction of high and low patient satisfaction hospital wards. The mean differences for all the independent variables except superior-subordinate relations corresponded to patient satisfaction. The tension in the low satisfaction ward was significantly higher than in the high satisfaction ward.

Patel and Srivastava (1978) conducted a study in the performance of 83 small enterprises in Gujarat in India to find out the relevance of managerial competence in the effectiveness of these organisations. Only percentages, mean and range were worked out to analyse data Result indicated that 32.5 per cent of the units having poor financial implication also had weak managers where as, stronger managerial abilities were associated with better financial performance. Higher managerial abilities were also related to trading experience and financial performance.

Mishra (1982) conducted a study in Government Corporations in India to find out the relationship between autonomy and effectiveness. The sample consisted of 56 officers and 94 non-officers. The data were obtained through the questionnaire method and correlation co-efficients were worked out. The result indicated that autonomy correlated positively with all dimensions of effectiveness. The autonomous organisations were more open to its employees. This reduced the delay in decision-making and provided intrinsic motivation to the employee leading to greater effectiveness.

Sayeed and Vishwanathan (1983) havestudied the relationship between job intrinsic and job extrinsic characteristics and organisational effectiveness in the manufacturing and non-manufacturing units of a technical institute. A sample survey was done on 188 respondents from the different units of the two organisations. Data were collected through Job Characteristics Scale and Effectiveness Scale adopted from Mott (1972). Mean, S.D. and relative ranking of job characteristics in two organisations were compared. Stepwise regression analysis between job characteristics factors and overall effectiveness was done. In the manufacturing companies the result indicated that job intrinsic as well as job extrinsic characteristics have relationship with organisational effectiveness. Job intrinsic factors like satisfaction and recognition from good work and job extrinsic characteristics like fairness of reward distribution system and morale of the worker showed significant relationship to organisational effectiveness. In non-manufacturing companies the relationship was found with job extrinsic factors, i.e. cooperation among workers, and morale. They, thus, concluded that job extrinsic factors were important determinant of organisational effectiveness.

Padaki (1984) conducted a study observing the relationship between the organisational climate, job satisfaction and organisational effectiveness. The study was conducted in the textile mills in Ahmedabad. Available measures of organisational climate and job satisfaction were used to measure climate and job satisfaction. An objective index of performance as developed by ATIRA which permits objective comparison of performance between various mills was used as a measure of organisational performance.

The data for climate, job satisfaction variables were obtained in the above study, from the employees of the organisations and were reduced to mean score and were ranked. Rank order correlation method was used to study the relationship between the satisfaction and climate. Two mills each, on the other hand, were grouped into most effective and least effective groups, and two groups were compared on various aspects of climate and satisfaction. The study showed more effective mills had higher score on all aspects of climate and effectiveness.

Sunderarajan (1984) conducted a comparative study of effectiveness in a private and a public sector organisations. The aim of the study was to find out the factors that contribute to effectiveness and the factors that account for significant differences in the two types of organisations. The independent factors studied were the hierarchy, decentralisation, control, communication, participation in decision-making, leadership styles and job involvement. The data were collected through the questionnaire and interviews. The result indicated that in the public sector, the management style and leadership were related to profit and turnover, and in the private sector decentralisation and job involvement were related to these factors. Some differences were also observed between managers of these organisation when grouped on the basis of age, work experience, frequency of promotions and type of job.

Singh and Paul (1985) tried to identify factors of excellence in Indian organisations. Findings were based on empirical research covering more than 1000 professional managers in public and private sector enterprises, government and academic institutions. To this, they have added content-analysis of the writings and statements of more than 1000 Indian chief executives and authors. Based on these efforts, they have identified the following four factors of effective management in India in their book 'Corporate Soul' : (i) Integrate internally by greater satisfaction and achievement of common goals by team work and building up of morale, (ii) Actuate and work for greater output through productivity improvement programme, (iii) Relate concern for customers and its public image, (iv) Create a climate of sustenance by relating talent and reducing alienation.

3

Effectiveness in Library Organisations

> "Libraries and reading are as vital to man in this Space Age as oxygen and breathing. Without the latter we fail physically, but without the former we are smoothered mentally and physically".
>
> Roger M. Blough : *Libraries and the Space Age*

Libraries as service organisations have played an important role in the development of man and his civilisation by preserving and transmitting the cultural heritage of ages. Butler (1933) feels that libraries have been created by actual necessities in the modern civilisation and have a vital societal role in its development. He expresses the view :

"Culture must transcend the individual whereby the man in each generation possesses, potentially at least, all that their predecessors have ever learned. Books are one social mechanism for preserving the racial memory and the library one special apparatus for transferring this to the consciousness of living individuals" (p. x).

Such all pervasive objectives of the libraries as being an 'apparatus of transmitting racial memory' are however, difficult to measure when put to test.

Library scientists have tried to assign more specific role to the libraries vis-a-vis the population they categorically serve. Dr. Ranganathan (1931), the father of library science in India, views libraries as growing organisms and as the focal point of all library operations. He emphasises that attempts should be made to fulfil their need for documents within minimum possible time, thus 'saving the time of the Readers'. In tnis process, the library will also achieve its other objectives : 'Every Book its' Reader and Every Reader its' Book'. Keeping in mind Dr. Ranganathan's stress on the users and the growth of the library organism, the objectives of the libraries may be defined as 'satisfaction of the users' and 'growth of the organisation'.

The role of the libraries vis-a-vis the readers they serve, received further emphasis at the hands of British library expert, McColvin. McColvin (1942) states that the library service exists to-serve-to give without question, favour or limitation. It is an instrument for the promotion of all or any of the activities of its readers.

Systems Perspective

Sydney Robert (1959) outlines the major factors that contribute to the success of a library system. He feels that a 'library depends for its success upon an efficient and enthusiastic librarian, supported by properly qualified staff, working in suitable premises'. Whereas McColvin puts emphasis on the satisfaction of users, Robert specifies how it could be achieved. His emphasis is on the factors that contribute to the success of the libraries. According to Robert, these are, efficient leadership, properly trained and placed staff, and suitable working conditions. Emphasis thus shifts from goals to the dynamics of the factors contributing to the achievement of the goals.

Later writers started viewing the libraries as systems, and defined an optimal system as one that transmits messages to recipients only so as to reduce the cost of transmitting such messages. The libraries become as vital as 'oxygen' and need proper utilization.

King and Bryant (1971) define libraries in the following manner :

> "Systems that transmit scientific and technical knowledge by means of document transfer system" (Quoted in Blagden, 1880 ; p. 27).

The documents include published material, research notes, magnetic tapes, or any other vehicle for storage of knowledge that may be transmitted from one individual to another. According to this definition, libraries are concerned with the transmission of knowledge. This definition fits well into the objectives of the academic and special libraries. These libraries, unlike public libraries, serve clientele who approach them with the specific goal of acquiring scholastic excellence.

King and Palmer (1973), commenting on the performance of such system, define an optimal library system as :

> ". . . would permit every message to be transmitted only to recipients who will use the information when the information is required at a cost that is less than or equal to be value of the information" (Quoted in Blagden, 1980 ; p. 14).

This definition provides for the evaluation of a library system in terms of cost-benefit analysis. Blagden (1980) thinks that it will mean assigning value to the use of library service. He, however, feels that the first priority should be in establishing a methodology for assessing the value of how well a library system is meeting users needs/corporate needs.

Blagden (1980) agrees with Burr (1975) who points out that organisations like individuals are multi-goal directed bodies ; defining corporate needs itself will prove complex and will complicate the evaluative process. Still he feels,in assessing overall performance of a library, users remain the focal point.

We may try to evaluate a library from the user's point of view by finding out how much satisfied they feel with its functioning.

Studies on Library Evaluation or Effectiveness

A study of the existing literature in the field reveals that the performance of the libraries have been reviewed mainly from three angles :

(a) The economic efficiency of the system,
(b) The value of the system to the users, and
(c) The effectiveness of the systems is the degree to which it achieves objectives.

Wessel (1967) and his co-workers attempted to develop criteria for evaluating a number of the United States Army Technical Libraries. In doing so, they developed a number of evaluative techniques, the important one being the SCORE.

SCORE (Service Components Reliability Efficiency) is a method of identifying the cost and success of various library functions. The technique is based on the analysis of each type of demand and the library's efficiency is measured by a time prescription. When such data are collected, forecasts regarding the probable future success can be made. This method of evaluation involves the economic efficiency of the system.

This technique assumes that each library operation can be calculated separately and compared in terms of the value of the demand met. Hawgood and Morley (1969) assert that libraries are complicated systems where everything interacts with everything else. There are certain physical resources and fixed budgets that make separate calculation of cost of each library operation difficult. Further, the technique discusses the input output variables but does not explain the dynamics of their interaction.

Hawgood and Morely (1969) based their study of performance evaluation of the libraries on the assumption that the library spends its funds in the most effective way and on the pattern of most desired activities. The blend of activities that a library is providing is compared with various alternative blends that can be produced. Each blend of activities signifies a certain pattern of weightage. The policy makers are presented with alternative weights, and if they prefer to review their weights, it means that a change in the activities is desired. They concluded in their study of Durham University Library that:

> Item of new stock was worth the same as
> Items of inter-library loans, or
> User's reference hours, or
> Items on long loan, or
> Hours of senior advice, or
> Hours of junior advice.

This model thus makes explicit the qualitative maximisation criteria and tries to assess the system on the basis of its efficiency. The model, however, does not throw light on how user's heeds are met. It rather attempts a maximisation of resource allocation on a pattern. The emphasis is on the input, but nothing is related to the output. It is also difficult to measure every library activity in terms of cost where each activity uses several resources and each research makes uses of several activities.

Wolfe (1970) and his co-workers conducted studies at Edinburgh with the object of developing a general methodology of evaluating non-profit organisations. They confined the study to the provision of information from the abstracts and journals. The services included title listing, selective dissemination of information etc. They based their study on the following assumptions (a) Scientists optimise their reading activities and will not read more than necessary, (b) Increase in secondary information doesn't reduce the output of the scientist, by way of diversion to wasteful activities, and (c) They assumed research production function in a particular form i.e·

$$R=f(S, I), S=E+N$$

where

> R=Research Output
> S=Scientific Output
> I=Information Input
> E=Scientific activity of the Researchers
> N=Information activity among them.

Based on these assumptions, they tried to establish a relation between information input and research output. They termed the information system effective, if it contributed to the increased research output. The data were collected through structured interviews from a sample of research scholars, librarian and budget allocators. The basic limitation of the study is that only a part of the system i.e. information system is taken. The evaluation technique is based on certain assumptions that may not be true.

Lancaster (1977) in evaluating a library system gives importance to user's needs and judges its efficiency in terms of its value to the users. In his attempt to give more objective tools of evaluation, he has developed the concept of 'Document Delivery System' against which the performance of a library can be judged. In his opinion, lists can be compiled from some standard sources of most commonly drawn citations and the capacity of the library to deliver the documents can be judged against it. Alternatively, actual needs of the users may be identified first by way of a survey, and then its capacity be judged against it.

A difficulty in applying this approach, in practice, may be that the users after knowing the strength and weakness of a library, may often turn to alternative sources for documents, rather than make their needs known to the library staff. Lancaster points out that when the scheme is attempted on a large library system the scanning system will become very cumbersome. The approach concentrates only on measurement of effectiveness.

Oldman (1978) conducted systematic studies on Cranefield Institute of Technology, and Loughbrough University of Technology. The study measured the performance of the libraries in terms of user's perception. Initial expectations of the users, before they had actually used the library, were first recorded and compared with their altered level of satisfaction, after the use. The derived value of satisfaction was obtained by the fo mula given below :

$$\text{Derived Value} = \frac{\text{Perceived Actualisation}}{\text{Expectation}}$$

This type of study can be attempted on a long term basis, where user's expectations are to be recorded before they actually make use of the library. It envisages a prior contact with the reader and cannot be operationalised over a short period of time.

Studies Conducted In India

In Indian literature, one rarely comes across studies on organisational effectiveness which attempt to analyse the behaviour in Indian libraries using multivariate criteria. In fact, very few studies like Sharma (1977) and Bhooshan Lal (1984), have tried to study the organisational problems in Indian libraries, but these studies do not touch upon the concept of effectiveness. Some of the Indian studies that deal with the organisational problems and users of the libraries are discussed below :

Sudame (1972) conducted a study to find out the effect of library use on the academic achievement of postgraduate students in Arts, Science and Education of M.S. University of Baroda. The independent variables selected for study were the qualifying examination, intelligence, socio-economic status, books taken for home reading, library familiarity with rules and regulation, time spent in library, books and journals received in the library, books owned, books received from other sources. Final examination marks were taken as a dependent variable.

Purposive sampling technique was used in choosing the respondents in first level of sampling. About 301 respondents formed the sample. Data were collected through a questionnaire and also from organisational records. Results were based on Mean, Standard, Deviation and Partial Regression analysis. The study establishes a positive relationship between the library use and academic achievement. The relationship was higher for the M. Sc. students than for the B. Ed. students. The most significant component of library use were books taken for home reading and familiarity with rules and regulation. The study establishes a relationship between the library use and academic achievements.

Sharma (1977) conducted a study to investigate the existing systems of all the ten universities in Madhya Pradesh (India) and the changes that have taken place so far vis-a-vis the response of the libraries, with a view to suggest methods of better organisation, management, financial system for university libraries. The instruments used were general information schedule and 3 sets of questionnaires for teachers, library staff and users. Representative sampling methods were used. 10 per cent of the total number of students, teachers, committee and council members were taken to form the sample. Only averages and percentages were worked out and data were tabulated and reported. The study was in the nature of a review of the functioning of the libraries in Madhya Pradesh. It was not intended to be a scientific study of the cause and effect relationship of different sets of variables to establish the validity of certain hypotheses.

Bhooshan Lal (1984) conducted a study on the performance of the library workers. Data were collected through various sets of questionnaires from 318 library personnel from twenty libraries in Delhi. The independent variables selected were demographic, psychological, organisational, and job-related. Mean. S.D., Correlations and Regression Analysis of the data were done to obtain the predictors of performance in libraries. The performance of the workers was measured by the heads of sections on performance appraisal performa. The result of the study indicated variables like responsibility, reward, esteemed need, identity, job satisfaction, type of organisation, job involvement as important correlation of performance. The result also indicated that the prediction of performance differed significantly at higher, middle, and lower job levels.

A review of the literature in library effectiveness reveals that most of the studies done in other countries concentrate on the methods of evaluating a library system or a part of it or they attempt to discover the criteria for such evaluation. Even among the criteria used for evaluation, the maximisation user's satisfaction, which has been clearly perceived as an important objective of the library (Burges 1970, Orr 1979; Blagden 1980), has not been adopted as a measure, except in the studies of Oldman (1978). These studies did not take into account the factors that contribute to better performance of library organisations and so did not fully explain the dynamics of their effective functioning.

Assessing service organisations becomes a difficult task because of their non-profit orientation. Perhaps, for this reason, few attempts have been made in India to study the concept of effectiveness in the context of library organisations by using a multiple criteria. Observing the gap in the field and keeping in view the importance of libraries as carriers of culture and information transmitting systems, the present study has been designed to study the concept of effectiveness in Indian libraries. It attempts to study the factors that contribute to their effective functioning and also the factors that can be adopted as measures of effectiveness in these organisations with special reference to academic and special libraries. The study will focus on (a) the internal systems of the libraries studied in terms of independent variables such a structure and task, policy, climate and employees behaviour, and (b) the feasible goals of the libraries such as, the user's satisfaction, employees's job satisfaction, performance of the group and rate of growth of the organisation.

Summary

A review of the literature has revealed that effectiveness has been assessed with reference to various criteria as shown in Table 3.1 The factors influencing effectiveness identified from amongst the studies have been listed in Table 3.2.

TABLE 3.1

Criteria (Measures) of Effectiveness

Criteria	Sources of Researchers
1. Growth	Katz and Kahn (1966), Negandhi and Reimann (1973), Child (1974, 1975).
2. Adaptability survival and control over environment	Katz and Kahn (1966), Yutchman and Seashore (1967), Price (1968), Osburn and Hunt (1974).
3. Goal achievement	Georgopoulos and Tennenbaum (1957), Argyris (1964), Campbell (1977), Steers (1977).
4. Satisfaction of different constituents or components of the system	Friedlander and Pickle (1968), Negandhi and Reimann (1973), Knowles (1975), Agrawal (1975), Porer et al. (1975), Van de Ven and Ferry (1980), Cameron (1981), Peters and Waterman (1982), Cummings (1983), Padaki (1984), Singh and Paul (1985).
5. Efficiency of process and organisational health	Bennis (1962), Beckhard (1969).
6. Group performance	Pearce and David (1983), Singh and Paul (1985)
7. Productivity	Blake and Mouton (1964), Mott (1972), Knowles (1975), Gilsson and Martin (1979).

TABLE 3.2

Correlates (Determinants) of Effectiveness

Correlates	Sources of Researchers
1. Size of the organisation	Sengupta (1969), Child (1974), Weiner and Mahoney (1981), Van de Ven and Ferry (1980).
2. Specialisation	Burns and Stalker (1961), Sengupta (1969), Negandhi and Reimann (1973). Van de Ven and Ferry (1980).
3. Supervisory levels/ Hierarchy	Negandhi and Reimann (1973), Van de Ven and Ferry (1980), Sunderarajna (1984).
4. Task and work procedures	Mott (1972), Osburn and Hunt (1974), Gilsson and Martin (1979), Van de Ven and Ferry (1980).
5. Policies of fairness of promotion	Sayeed and Vishwanathan (1983), Padaki (1984), Sunderarajan (1983).
6. Decision making and participation	Burns and Stalker (1961), Negandhi and Reimann (1973), Weiner and Mahoney (1981), Padaki (1984). Sunderarajan (1984).
7. Leadership style and communication pattern	Burns and Stalker (1961), Agrawal (1975), Steers (1977), Patel and Srivastava (1978), Weiner and Mahoney (1981), Padaki (1984), Goldsmith and Clutterbuck (1985), Sunderarajan (1984).
8. Inter-unit coordinations	Mott (1972), Agrawal (1975), Van de Ven and Ferry (1980).

4

Theoretical Framework

The present chapter addresses itself, briefly, to the various approaches and theoretical frameworks adopted by the researchers on organisational effectiveness and discusses in detail the framework underlying the present study.

Approaches (Models) of Effectiveness

Different approaches and models that have been used in evaluating the effectiveness of the organisations are briefly described below:

Goal Approach

Under this approach, the organisation is assessed in terms of its stated goals. The goals, can be productivity, rate of profit, or the satisfaction of certain groups. The approach is useful when the organisation has clearly defined goals which can be operationalised. The approach has been adopted by Etzioni (1960), Price (1968) and Campbell (1977).

System Approach

Under this approach the effectiveness of the organisation is measured in terms of its capability to acquire resources and utilize them for achieving the organisational objectives. It studies the input output relation in an interlinked manner. This approach has been used by Argyris (1964), Katz and Kahn (1966), Yutchman and Seashore (1967), Schneider (1983), Veldsman (1984).

Internal Process Approach

This approach judges the effectiveness, in terms of efficacy of internal process of the organisation. If the organisation has smooth functioning of communication, decision-making and control processes, it will be indicative of a healthy and free of strain organisational set-up. Bennis (1962, Steers 1977) make use of this approach.

Strategic Constituency Approach

The effectiveness of the organisation is studied by judging the extent to which an organisation satisfies the demand and expectations of its constituents. The constituents have powerful influence on the operations of the organisation. Friendlander and Pickle (1968) and Cameron (1981) have made use of this approach.

It is not essential, however, that the researcher has to adopt a particular approach only. When we study the concept in totality a system view emerges. But we do study the goals of the system and its various processes to understand how the system realises its objectives, and in this manner different approaches are combined to have a broader perspective.

Normative and Descriptive Models

Viewing from another angle, the models adopted for studying organisational effectiveness can be classified as normative or as descriptive models. Normative models attempt to specify things that an organisation must do to become effective, that is to prescribe the desirable behaviour. Descriptive models, on the other hand, summarise those characteristics that have been found in successful organisations. Generally, the resear-

have adopted normative models, however, the studies like 'In search of excellence' by Peters and Waterman (1982) and 'Winning Streak' by Goldsmith and Clutterbuck (1985) highlight descriptive models.

Univariate and Multivariate Models

Researchers have analysed the concept of organisational effectiveness using either univariate or multivariate measures. Initial attempts have been in terms of univariate measure such as profit, turnover, productivity. Subsequently, it was realised that a single criterion is not sufficient to encompass complex organisational behaviour. Criterion like productivity or absenteeism alone cannot explain whether an organisation is achieving its major goals and progressing towards healthier growth. Authors like Georgopolous and Tennenbaum (1957) made initial attempts to measure effectiveness using multivariate measures. The approach since then has been adopted by several authors.

Some Theories of Organisational Effectiveness

The review of literature under Chapter 2 reveals that there is a wealth of theories on organisational effectiveness, yet there is no consensus among the researchers regarding the approaches criteria and correlates of organisational effectiveness. However, as discussed earlier in this chapter, a systems perspective emerges out more clearly when we view the organisations in their totality. The views of a few authors who have studied the concept in this perspective are discussed below :

Argyris (1964) defines effectiveness of the organisation in terms of achievement of its core activities. According to him an organisation is effective if it achieves three core activities : (a) achieving objectives, (b) maintaining the internal system, (c) and adapting itself to external environment with a decreasing or constant input, while maintaining or increasing the output of the system.

Argyris (1964) emphasis the systems approach to the concept of effectiveness and states that interrelatedness among the elements of the system should be focused. For example, the accomplishment of objectives may mean co-ordinating the role of man, machines and their integration with informal behaviour. The internal system of an organisation would include all formal and informal activities of authority and controls such as communication, training, budgets, incentives. In adapting itself to the environment, the organisational activities of sales, public relations, legal and governmental relations, would be included. The effectiveness of the organisation has to be seen by judging how various activities of the organisation are integrated and maintained and oriented towards its goals. Argyris has hypothesised that there is incongruence between the individual and organisation. If an organisation can provide an individual with an opportunity by which he is able to define his goals and relate them to the goals of the organisation, the incongruence can become the basis for continued challenge which will help the man to enhance his growth and develop organisations which are viable and effective. The organisation has to adopt such problem-solving processes that render minimum damage to effectiveness.

Katz and Kahn (1966) have analysed the concept from different frames of reference. Viewing it from the organisational point of view, organisational effectiveness, according to them means maximisation of return to the organisation by all means. The means adopted to achieve maximisation of returns may be technical means and non-economic or political means. Thus, 'maximisation' is determined by the combination of efficiency of the organisation as a system, which is defined as the ratio of energy output to energy input (technical means) ; and the success of the organisation in obtaining on advantageous terms the input it requires, which may be termed as political effectiveness (non-economic means). In the short run, organisational effectiveness is a combination of efficiency and political effectiveness.

In the long run the organisations will display the characteristics of (1) Growth, (2) Survival, (3) Storage, (4) Control over the external environment. In their words, effectiveness will then be synonymous with these terms.

They further state :

> "Increase in effectiveness by both means are typically observable as storage of energy, organisational growth, organisational endurance, survival and organisational control of surrounding environment" (p. 170).

Defining the organisation from an individual member's frame of reference, Katz and Kahn define as the most effective organisation that which offers the greatest aggregate returns to its member.

From the organisational and individual frames of reference they take the concept to the supersystem, the society, of which the organisation is a part and assess it in terms of the effectiveness of thc entire social system and state :

> "Effectiveness would be assessed in terms of organisational contribution to efficiency, survival power and environmental control of the entire social system.' (p. 166).

In contrast to the traditional theorists, Katz and Kahn look at social organisations as open systems. They maintain that in a social organisation conversion of output into further energic input consists of transactions between the organisation and its environment and this makes it an open system. They feel that an open system by virtue of its importation of greater energy from the environment does not run down where as a closed system may tend towards such a state after the equilibrium has been reached. The basic paradigms of an open system model are depicted in Figure 1.

They have suggested nine characteristics that are common to all open systems.

Characteristics of Open Systems

Importation of energy (input) from the external environment.

Transformation of energy (throughout) by means of work activity.

Exportation of transformed energy (outputs) to the external environment.

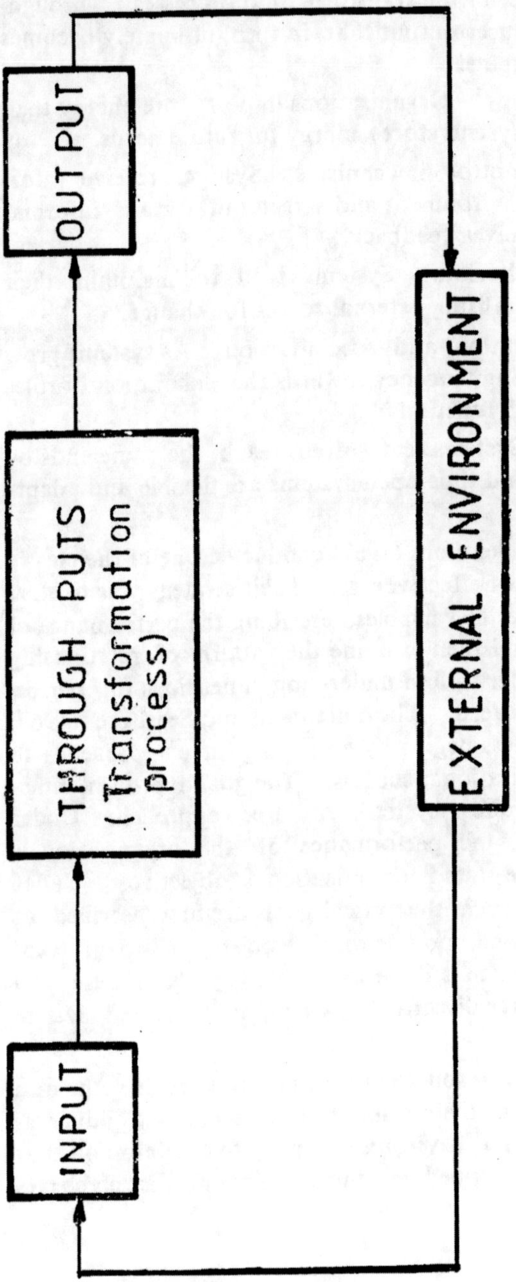

FIG.1: PARADIGM FOR AN OPEN SYSTEM MODEL.
Source:- Steers : Organisatinal Effectivenes
A behavioural approach (p-10)

Cyclic character of the transformation processes : Throughout activities produces output that, in turn, ultimately becomes sources for new inputs.

Negative entropy : Organisations import more energy than they export, thus system stores energy for future needs.

Information control mechanisms : Systems receive information from the environment and screen out certain information and again receives feedback.

Steady state behaviour: Systems tend to maintain their behaviour by neutralising external forces for change.

Role differentiation and specialisation : As systems grow there is an increasing tendency towards the elaboration of roles in specialisation of functions.

Equifinality : Systems can often reach the same ends by different means and thus open systems are flexible and adaptable.

Yutchman and Seashore (1967) conducted one of the classic studies in the area of effectiveness. Their strategy was to start with a large number of variables describing the performance of the organisation and then examine the pattern of relationship among them in order to find underlying dimensions of performance from this pattern. The Yutchman and Seashore (1967) model of effectiveness begins by proposing three approaches to the study or organisational success. The goal approach, functional approach and system resource approach. Under the first approach, the performance of the organisation is compared with pre-stated organisational objectives. Under the functional approach, theoretical goals are first ascribed to the organisation based upon its role in society, and then comparison of performance is done with these goals. These two approaches were later discarded by them, and adopted system resource approach.

Under the system resource model, effectiveness is defined in terms of the ability of the organisation to secure an advantageous position in its environment and to capitalise on that position to acquire valued resources. They further elaborate by stating the following :

> "The concept of 'bargaining position' implies the exclusion of any specific goal (or function) as the ultimate criterion of organisational effectiveness. Instead it points to the more general capability of the organisation as a resource-getting system" (p. 898).

They, however, emphasise optimising the returns from the environment rather than maximising them.

The systems models, as proposed by these authors in terms of input-output (Argyris, 1964), maximisation of returns (Katz and Kahn, 1966) and organisation as resource getting systems (Yutchman and Seashore, 1967), may be easy to operationalise in profit making organisations. But these cannot be adopted as a framework of analysis in evaluating service organisations where there may not be any direct link between the input and output of the organisation and where maximisation of return to the users rather than the organisation may be the objective. Here, a much simpler approach to effectiveness—in terms of achievement of its goals is called for. Such a framework has been provided by Steers (1977) who defines effectiveness in terms of the achievement of operational goals as well lays emphasis on different sub-systems of the organisations such as structure, environment, employee and the manager. Steers (1977) model of effectiveness and the framework underlying the present study are discussed in detail in the forthcoming discussion.

Framework Underlying the Present Study

The present study, based on Steers (1977) views on effectiveness, attempts to evaluate service organisations in terms of achievement of their goals. This process of goal achievement is viewed in a systems perspective where interrelatedness among different components of the system such as, structure, climate, employee and managerial policies and the goals is studied to find out what contributes to the success of a service organisation. The study thus combines the systems and goal approach to effectiveness. Steers (1977) definition of effectiveness has been adopted for the purpose of analysis.

Operational Definition

Steers (1977) defines the organisation as :

> ". . . .Complex entities that strive for rational allocation of resources for the purpose of goal attainment" (p. 2).

He defines effectiveness as follows:

> "...Organisations capacity to acquire and utilize its scarce valued resources as expeditiously as possible in pursuit of its operative and operational goals" (p. 5).

In this definition he defines goals an operational or feasible goals. The emphasis is not on maximisation of returns to the organisation by all means (Katz and Kahn, 1966) but on optimisation of goals. He stresses this point by stating :

> "Thus, effectiveness is evaluated in terms of how well organisation can attain its feasible goals" (p. 5).

By emphasising the optimal and not the maximisational nature of the goals, Steers definition allows for the 'multiple, often conflicting goals, as well as the existence of several constraints on goal effort'. For example, the goal of profit maximisation and employees satisfaction may be contradictory in the short run. Also if a firm's production goals are maximised at the cost of its research development, or employee's satisfaction, the long term survival of the firm may be in danger. There may also be several constraints of money, technology, and personnel that may slow down the goal maximisation attempts of the organisation. Steers definition appears realistic because he believes that the greater the progress that is made towards such goals, the more effective is the organisation.

The goals as seen by Steers (1977) are not static but subject to change over time as the goal attainment depends upon the 'organisation's capacity to acquire and utilise its scarce and valued resources'.

The important resources available at the disposal of the organisations are : monetary, technical and human. Their expeditious utilization will depend on 'various factors operating within and outside the organisations. The factors within the organisations may be structural, such as the size of the organisation, degree of specialisation, supervisory levels, and supervisory-staff ratios ; the task distribution pattern ; the policies of the organisation ; the factors indicating the climate of the organisation, the state of inter-unit coordination and the employee factor reflecting his job behaviour. Steers has perceived goal attainment by the organisations within the framework of dynamics of these factors in the organisation and the external environment as they relate to each other and utimately affect the goal directed effort. He has thus seen the organisational effectiveness in a systems perspective.

In his study of dynamics of organisational effectiveness, Steers (1977) has laid specific emphasis and the behaviour of the employee. Explaining this he states ;

> "In addition to the structural, technological and environmental influence on effectiveness, perhaps the most direct contribution to the organisational success comes from the behaviour of the employees themselves. It is the employee who constitute an organisations structure and make use of organisations technologies. Moreover, it is the employees who respond to environmental variations and pressure... Organisational success lies in the manner in which the members of the organisation work together (or fail to work together) for goal attainment" (p. 113-114).

Steers concurrs with Katz and Kahn (1966) when he states that the following three important behavioural requirements must be met in order to ensure the ultimate success of the organisation. These are ;

1. Organisation should be able to attract and maintain a flow of qualified manpower by offering them suitable rewards by way of promotion and training policies.
2. The employee should primarily perform the task for which he is recruited and is responsible. Therefore, the organisation must secure dependable role performance by assigning suitable tasks and defining their roles clearly.
3. In addition, successful organisations also require that employee engage in innovative behaviour, has

autonomy of work, feels involved in the jobs, and maintains high standard of job.

Effectiveness Defined in Terms of Goal Achievement

The present study, in view of Steers (1977) definition discussed above, outline the following multiple goals which a library organisation may strive to achieve :

A consistent increase in its economic resources over a period of time-reflecting its capacity to acquire resources. This may be reflected in the rate of increase in the budget of the organisation.

To receive dependable role performance from its employees. In a library organisation work proceeds in an inter-linked manner from one unit to another unit. Its objective can be defined as securing dependable role performance from different task groups.

To allow its employees to draw a good deal of satisfaction from their jobs so that they may engage in innovative behaviour and develop attachment to the organisation. Without attachment and performance, effectiveness becomes all but impossible'. (Steers, 1977).

To attempt for maximisation of library use and user's satisfaction (Burges, 1970). The libraries are service organisations and satisfaction of users is their ultimate objective. The attainment of earlier goals of growth, performance and job satisfaction can represent inputs into the determination of subsequent goals (Steers, 1977), in this case the user's satisfaction.

The present study looks at organisational effectiveness as a multidimensional concept. The goal achievements of the libraries, as outlined in the foregoing, discussion is attempted to be measured by the following variables :

Variables Measuring Effectiveness

1. User's satisfaction.
2. Employee's job satisfaction.
3. Performance of the group
4. Rate of growth of the organisation.

Detailed discussion of these variables will follow under the heading "variables measuring effectiveness".

Variables Influencing Effectiveness

The organisational effectiveness thus measured is assumed to be influenced by various factors operating within and outside the organisation. The following independent variables have been chosen for the present study.

Structural

(i) Size of the Organisation
(ii) Degree of Specialisation (No. of sections)
(iii) Supervisory Levels (Hierarchy)
(iv) Supervisory-staff Ratios.

Task

(i) Reporting and Work Distribution
(ii) Placement
(iii) Work Procedures.

Policy

(i) Reward and Punishment
(ii) Training
(iii) Performance Appraisal

Collection—Size of library collection

Inter-unit Coordination

Climate

(i) Leadership Style
(ii) Communication
(iii) Decision-making

Employees Job Behaviour

(i) Job Characteristics
(ii) Background Characteristics
(iii) Job Affiliation

These correlates or determinants of effectiveness are being described in detail in the forthcoming discussion in this chapter under the heading 'Correlates of Effectiveness.

The Systems Perspective and Model Adopted for Study

The present study which has operationalised Steers (1977) definition of effectiveness for the purpose of analysing library organisations, attempts to investigate them in a systems perspective. As discussed earlier, researchers like Argyris (1964), Katz and Kahn (1966) and Yutchman and Seashore (1967) have proposed systems model for evaluating organisations. In the model adopted for the study, the emphasis is on the interrelatedness of the various parts of the systems as they together contribute to effectiveness. Etzioni (1964) feels that a systems model of effectiveness :

> "Defines a pattern of inter-correlations among the elements of the systems which would make it most effective in the service of a given goal as compared to other combinations of the same or similar elements" (p. 19).

Schein (1976) also highlights the interrelatedness of the various dimensions of the organisation and states that effectiveness cannot be ensured by emphasising any particular aspect of the organisation. Rather, the total system has to be viewed. Steers (1977) has also perceived the goal attainment of the organisations within the framework of dynamics of factors operating within and outside the organisation as they relate to each other and ultimately affect the goal directed effort.

The present study, being a study of organisational effectiveness from short-time frame of reference, lays emphasis on the dynamics of the internal system of the organisation, rather than its external environment. This model adopted for depicting the effectiveness is given in Figure-2. The various components i.e. inputs of the model are linked with each other and together they contribute to the effectiveness which is being measured by four different sets of variables. The effectiveness of the system again has its impact on the components of the system. The model thus reflects a dynamic process of organisation behaviour.

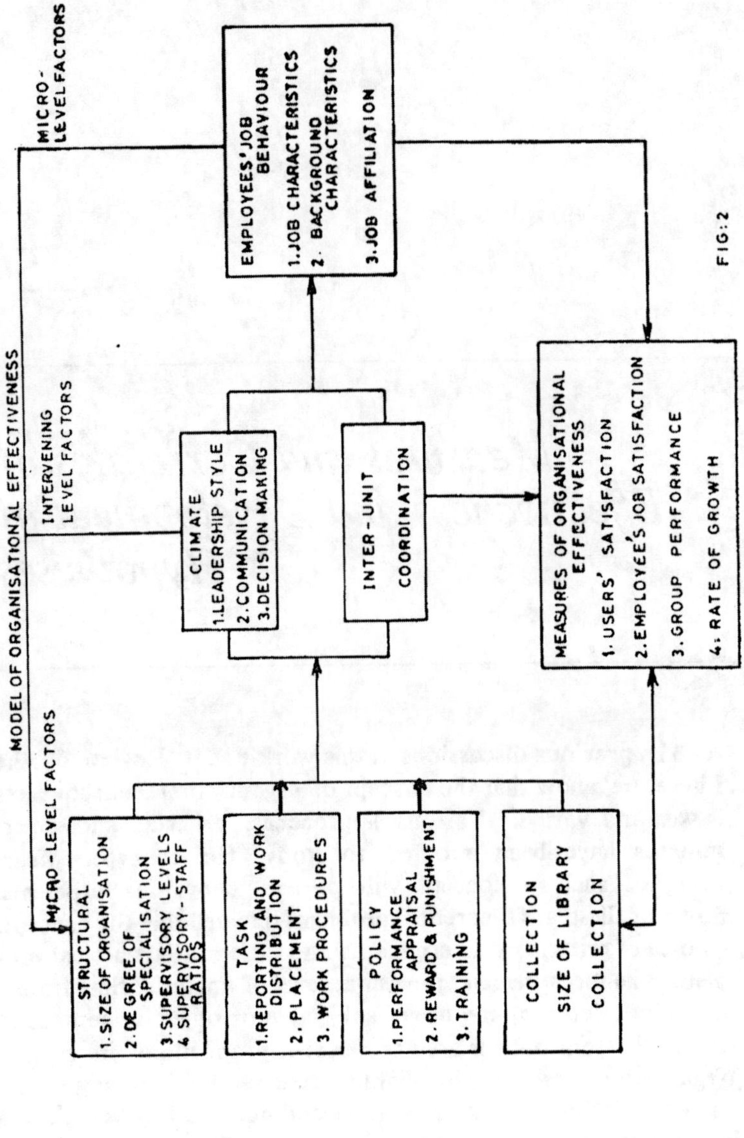
MODEL OF ORGANISATIONAL EFFECTIVENESS
MICRO-LEVEL FACTORS
INTERVENING LEVEL FACTORS
MICRO-LEVEL FACTORS
STRUCTURAL
1. SIZE OF ORGANISATION
2. DEGREE OF SPECIALISATION
3. SUPERVISORY LEVELS
4 SUPERVISORY- STAFF RATIOS
TASK
1. REPORTING AND WORK DISTRIBUTION
2. PLACEMENT
3. WORK PROCEDURES
POLICY
1. PERFORMANCE APPRAISAL
2. REWARD & PUNISHMENT
3. TRAINING
COLLECTION
SIZE OF LIBRARY COLLECTION
CLIMATE
1. LEADERSHIP STYLE
2. COMMUNICATION
3. DECISION MAKING
INTER-UNIT COORDINATION
EMPLOYEES' JOB BEHAVIOUR
1. JOB CHARACTERISTICS
2. BACKGROUND CHARACTERISTICS
3. JOB AFFILIATION
MEASURES OF ORGANISATIONAL EFFECTIVENESS
1. USERS' SATISFACTION
2. EMPLOYEE'S JOB SATISFACTION
3. GROUP PERFORMANCE
4. RATE OF GROWTH

FIG:2

5

Measures and Correlates of Effectiveness and Development of Hypotheses

The previous discussions in this work under 'Review of the Literature' show that the concept of organisational effectiveness is vast and varied. Various approaches, criteria, and determinants have been adopted to study the concept. Measuring of such a concept will present enormous problems. Some of these are theoretical problems like defining the concept. Choice of criteria or determinants and others are practical problems like measurement precision, level of analysis, time frame, frame of reference, and use of subjective or objective sources of data. These problems assume serious proportions in service organisations which are characterised by wide ranging goals, un clear relationship between means and ends and weak linkages between units. A researcher evaluating the library organisations cannot ignore these problems.

The review of library literature has revealed that a wide variety of criteria have been adopted to evaluate the library organisations. The cost-benefit criteria have been adopted by Wessel (1967), Hawgood and Morely (1969); the value of systems approach is reflected in the studies of Wolfe (1970) and Lancaster (1977) and an attempt to measure effectiveness in terms of user's perception is made by Oldman (1978). A study in library effectiveness has to be carefully designed with reference to the choice of criteria for evaluation. This study has adopted multiple criteria for evaluating the libraries.

While analysing the library organisations, a researcher also encounters the controversy regarding the use of subjective or objective data. Orr (1979) states that the most commonly employed indicators of values in libraries are the measures of utilization (figures) as given in the annual reports (objective data). But he also feels that these are not so useful. To these, he prefers a global measure of total value of library service to the users (subjective data). The present study makes use of subjective as well as objective sources of data.

Hall et al. (1967) report that service organisations are most complex and it is not easy to measure their performance. The problem of assessing the organisation on the basis of their goal achievement becomes more complicated among different types of organisations.

Perrow (1967) states :

> "... Types of organisations in terms of their function in society will vary as much within each type as between types. Thus, some schools, hospitals, banks, and steel companies may have in common, because of their routine character, than routine and non-routine schools, routine and non-routine hospitals and so-forth" (p. 203).

The present study, while attempting to measure the effectiveness under a comparative reference in special and academic libraries, recognises such constraints in comparing the performance of two different types of libraries. For example, it may be true that an academic library primarily caters to the routine type of information needs of the students and the faculty whereas a special library normally engages itself in the non-routine type of retrieval. This may account for the differences in their functioning. Yet, their goals can be commonly defined and common measures of evaluating them can be adopted, as their basic orientation is the same i.e. the satisfaction of the users.

Variables Measuring Effectiveness in Libraries

In the present study, the following variables have been adopted as measures of effectiveness on the basis of studies cited under each :

1. User's Satisfaction
2. Employee's Job Satisfaction
3. Performance of the Group
4. Rate of Growth of the Organisation

User's Satisfaction

Effectiveness of the Organisations has been assessed in terms of the satisfaction of the system's components or constitutents like users employees, customers and owners by Friedland and Pickle (1968), Agarwal (1975), Negandhi and Reimann (1973), Van de Ven and Ferry (1980), Cameron (1981) and Padaki (1984). Library scientists, particularly Wolfe (1970), Lancaster (1977), Oldman (1978) and Orr (1979) have adopted users' need, demand or satisfaction as criteria for evaluating library organisations.

Drucker (1973) maintains that the primary difference between a service institution like a library and a business organisation is that the business organisations receives resources by satisfying the customer, and the service institution is supported by a budget allocation from a funding source. Because the funding source and the user's of the organisation are separated, a service institution has little direct relationship between the input and the output of the organisation. According to him, a library can be evaluated in terms of whether it is capable of satisfying the users demand by providing the necessary information or material ; what the user subsequently does with this material is outside the librarian's control.

Burges (1970) states that the three major concern of a library should be : (a) Maximisation of library usage, (b) Reasons for non-use of library by certain members, (c) User's satisfaction and creation of conducive working environment. Orr (1979) recommends evaluation of library on the basis of its value to users and states :

> "The librarian's ideal tool for justification task would be a global measure of the total value of the library service representing sum of values attributed to all uses of services" (p. 320).

Hannabuss (1983) states that there are conceptional difficulties in adopting the quantitative measure for evaluating the library usage. A criterion like the availability of the document may mean its being locatable, identifiable or deliverable. Sincilarly, the utilisation of documents may mean scanning, referring or making their use for citing references. He holds the view that :

> "It is much easier to measure the recall, currency and precision of information provided, say by an on-line data base service, than the value of benefit to a group of users throughout an academic session, it is even easier to measure cost per minute spent on-line searches" (p. 420).

Besides conceptual difficulties, there may be problems of selecting the appropriate dimensions for measuring the users' satisfaction. This, however, should not prevent a researcher in adopting it as a measure of effectiveness in library organisaations. In the present study, the user's satisfaction has been measured by 'Users' Satisfaction Scale' (Appendix-B).

Employee's Job Satisfaction

Employee's job satisfaction has been adopted as a measure of organisational effectiveness by Negandhi and Reimann (1973), Van de Ven and Ferry (1980), Sayeed and Vishwanathan (1983), Padaki (1984). Van de Ven and Ferry (1980) states ;

> "Job satisfaction is an effective reaction or feeling by an employee on how happy or satisfied he or she feels with the job, supervisor, co-worker, pay, and his/her current and future career progress and potential" (p. 390).

This effective reaction' is related to the achievement of a unique pattern of the needs and goals of the employee. Porter et al. (1975) view the satisfaction of the personal needs and goals of the employee as one of the objectives of an organisation. They maintain that every individual enters the organisation with some expectations and also brings with him his skill and energies. The organisation has its resources to offer as rewards to the individuals. The individuals will value and seek to maintain the membership of the organisation to the extent to which they find its membership and involvement serving or satisfying their own needs or felicitating the achievement of their goals.

Thus, the satisfaction of the needs of employee by the organisation, particularly, the employees satisfaction from the job, becomes an important indicator of organisational effectiveness. Though there exists a controversy in the literature regarding job satisfaction and performance relationship, the studies by Van de Ven and Ferry (1980) and Padaki (1984) have shown positive relationship between organisational effectiveness and employee's job satisfaction. In the present study it has been measured by 'Job Satisfaction Scale' (Appendix-C)

Group Performance

By studying the work group, we can understand better the behaviour and decisions of the individuals and the structure of the total organisations (Shull, Delbecq and Cummings, 1970). Van de Ven and Ferry (1980) state :

> "The organisational unit represents the basic (and smallest) building block for examining the collective behaviour. . ." (p. 155).

Formal groups in an organisation are, normally, formed on the basis of the tasks. Every organisation requires some division of labour and has departments, divisions or units to accomplish the tasks. Defining the work of the individual sub-systems and ensuring that their work is integrated towards the goal of the organisation as a whole is a key factor that determines the effectiveness (Cohen, 1980). Bardford (1980) holds the view :

> "The effective formation of group and its continued development requires time and patience. It requires active effort on the part of the leader to produce an atmosphere of trust and involvement of group members in the functioning of the group. . . By indicating through word and action the necessary group task and maintenance roles, a leader can encourage members to assume these roles whenever appropriate" (p. 8).

The performance of the group will thus be greatly influenced by the structural, task and coordination variables. The policies of the organisation, the leadership styles and communication channels, and employees behaviour will have a significant relationship with the performance of the group.

In a library organisation, the final product, i.e. the service to the users, is obtained through a series of inter-linked tasks of highly interdependent groups. For example, the documents produced by Acquisition Department are forwarded to Processing Department ; the processed documents are then forwarded to Service Department for shelving and circulation. In such a work organisation, the performance of the different groups has an important role in the overall functioning of the library. The effective functioning of the groups will reflect the efficiency with which the library serves its users. The group performance thus emerges as an important dimension of library effectiveness and is adopted as a measure of effectiveness in the present study. The performance of the group is being measured by the Group Performance Scale (Appendix-D).

Rate of Growth (Financial Indicator)

Generally, the growth of a country or of an organisation is measured in economic terms. The rate of growth refers to the average rate at which a nation or an organisation increases its resources over a period of time. The budget of an organisation is an economic indicator of its capacity to grow, survive and adapt. The rate of growth of the budget indicates whether this capacity is substantial and sustained.

The literature on effectiveness displays a controversy regarding the use of subjective/objective data. The present study makes use of subjective as well as objective data for analysing effectiveness. The rate of increase in the budget of an organisation is an objective datum which is used as one of the indicators of effectiveness in this study. Effectiveness has been viewed in terms of organisational growth by Katz and Kahn (1966), Negandhi and Reiniann (1973), Child (1974).

Van de Ven (1980) suggested the following characteristics for effectiveness criteria : (a) They should be concrete indicators or organisational effectiveness, (b) be easiest to measure, (c) show wide variations in different organisations. The rate of growth variable fully meets these requirements. The increase in the budget is worked out over a period of three years as data were not available for longer comparable period. The information was obtained from the organisational records, annual reports etc. and was compiled separately for each library.

Correlates of Effectiveness

The correlates chosen for studying the effectiveness are presented as Macro-level factors, Intervening-level factors and Micro-level factors. The variables chosen for study under each are depicted in Table 5.1 and are described below :

Macro-Level Factors

Strutural

(a) Size of the Organisation

(b) Degree of Specialization
(Number of Sections)

(c) Supervisory Levels (Hierarchy)

(d) Supervisory-Staff Ratio

TABLE 5.1

Correlates of Organisational Effectiveness

Macro-Level Variables	Intervening-Level Variables	Micro-level Variables
1. Structural	5. Climate	7. Employees Job Behaviour
(i) Size of Organisation	(i) Leadership Styles	(i) Job Characteristics
(ii) Degree of Specialisation (Nos. of section)	(ii) Communication	(ii) Background Characteristics
(iii) Supervisory levels (Hierarchy)	(iii) Decision-Making	(iii) Job Affiliation
(iv) Supervisory-Staff Ratio		
2. Task	6. Inter-Unit Coordination	
(i) Reporting and Work Distribution		
(ii) Placement		
(iii) Work Procedure		
3. Policy		
(i) Performance Appraisal		
(ii) Reward/Punishment		
(iii) Training		
4. Collection		
Size of Library Collection		

Task

(a) Reporting and Work distribution
(b) Placement
(c) Work Procedures

Policy

(a) Performance Appraisal
(b) Reward and Punishment
(c) Training

Collection

(a) Size of the Library Collection

Intervening-Level Factor

Climate

(a) Leadership Style
(b) Communication
(c) Decision-Making

Inter-unit Coordination

Micro-Level Factors
Employee's Job Behaviour

(a) Job Characteristics
(b) Background Characteristics
(c) Job Affiliation

The organisational behaviour that ultimately reflects the effectivity or non-effectivity of the system is caused by the interaction of highly complex systems of the organisation (Macro-level variables) and the individual (Micro-level variables) (Luthans, 1972). The intervening variables representing the internal state of the organisation (Likert, 1961) influence the dynamics of individual and organisational interactions. Studies by Marrow et al. (1967) and Lawler et al. (1974) have specifically explored and established the intervening role of organisational climate. Within this simple framework, the variables for the study have been chosen on the basis of their relevance to the concept of effectiveness in library organisations. The variables selected, along with the research reviews cited under the studies and further research evidence in support of each variable, have been discussed in the forthcoming analysis. The study on interdependence of organisational variables conducted by Franklin (1975) was of particular interest in the choice of determinants of effectiveness for the present study.

Structural Variables

At the macro-level the organisational structural problems tend to be operationalised in terms of the optimum size, decision on horizontal and vertical division of labour reflected by the degree of specialisation and supervisory levels, and the appropriate level of administrative span of control (Van de Ven and Ferry, 1980). Factors like the size of the organisation, type, nature of ownership possibly effect performance (Roos et al., 1974). The data for structural variables chosen for this study have been taken from organisational records and by interviewing the senior members of the staff where required.

Size of the Organisation

The conventional approach to measure the size of an organisation is to count the number of people in the organisational chart (Blau, Schoenherr, 1971), (Hickson et al, 1971), (Hall et al., 1967). In this study, the size has been measured by counting the number of employees from the organisational Record Profile prepared for each organisation. The organisations have been classified into large, medium and small, depending upon the number of employees working in them.

Van de Ven and Ferry (1980) state that increasing organisational size is negatively correlated with job satisfaction because more impersonal methods of administration are necessary among greater number of people where individual contributions become annonymous. Some other researchers feel that the members of small organisations report greater responsibility, involvement which may ultimately influence their performance (Barker and Gump, 1964), (Wicker, 1968), (Wicker and Mehler, 1971). Raven (1959) found a negative correlation between the efficiency and size in coal mines, when the size increased above a certain level. However, mixed and insignificant relationships have been found among some studies that directly related size to various measures or organisational productivity or goal attainment. On the basis of the above studies, a negative relationship between the size of the organisation and organisational effectiveness is postulated.

Degree of Specialisation

One of the basic thrusts in industrialised societies is to increase the degree of specialisation and intensify divison of labour which will result in increased productivity due to innovation, creativity, and reduced labour costs. However, specialisation has also been shown to be related to increased friction and conflict within organisation. Melcher (1976) states specialisation sharply increase the complexity both in society and organisation and its immediate effect is to create inter-dependence workers and groups. Each specialist must fulfil his responsibility so that overall job can be done. A completely interdependent relationship is created when the output of one position becomes the input of another. The relationship depicted in Figure 3 is particularly relevant to library organisations where the output of one unit serves as the input of another unit.

Specialisation may be measured in a number of ways including the number of divisions within an organisation or number of specialists within each division (Hall, 1972), number of different sub-units in an organisation (Blau and Schoenherr, 1971). The present study measured it in terms of different units existing in an organisation.

It is, generally, assumed that increased specialisation will lead to increased effectiveness because it allows each employee to operate in a particular area so as to maximise his or her contribution to goal directed activities. Steers (1977) states that specialisation may be beneficial in terms of employees' performance, but it may, simultaneously, be deterimental to employees in terms of their job attitude, mental health and propensity to remain in the organisation. Melcher (1976) states that a completely interdependent relationship created out of division of labour creates strain on relationships. In a library organisation, where task interdependence is high, the functioning cannot be optimised without improving the functioning of all other units. Such inter-dependent nuture of work will also have adverse implication for performance and job satisfaction.

The studies that have measured organisational effectiveness in terms of reduced costs (Blau et al, 1966) have shown positive relationship between the specialisation and organisational effectiveness. However, the studies adopting the reduced conflict as criterion of effectiveness have found negative relationship between specialisation and organisational effectiveness

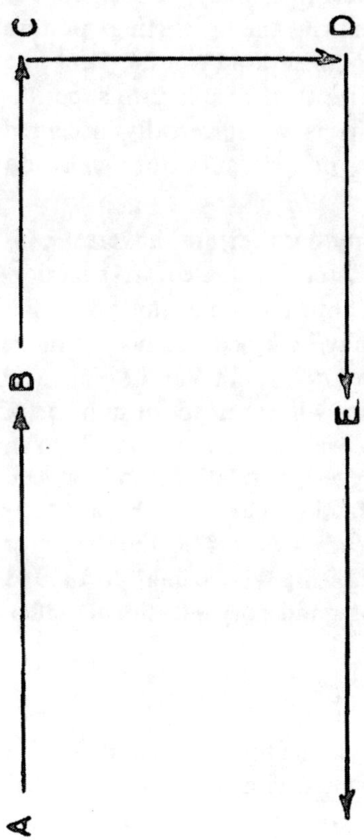

FIG. 3 Interdependent workflow

Source MELCHER : STRUCTURE AND PROCESSE OF ORGANISATION A SYSTEMATIC APPROACH (p-62)

(Child, 1973). In the present study, in view of the interdependent nature of the tasks to be performed by the library personnel, a negative relationship between specialisation as reflected in the number of sections and effectiveness is postulated.

Supervisory Levels (Hierarchy)

The number of supervisory levels (hierarchy) refers to the different strata that are manifest in the reporting pattern between formal positions in the organisation (Van de Ven and Ferry, 1980). Hierarchy, arrangement of people into superior-subordinate chain of relationship is a universally accepted principle of management, and no organisation can do without it.

Hierarchy, though essential, produces certain adverse consequences when under its guise tension is created in superior-subordinate relations and when channels of communication are obstructed, employee's initiative may be killed because of more emphasis on conformity. Coutler (1979) and Van de Ven and Ferry (1980) have conducted studies where impact of number of supervisory levels on effectiveness was studied. Van de Ven and Ferry (1980) reported a negative relationship between levels of supervision and job satisfaction which had been adopted as one of the measures of effectiveness. On the basis of above studies, a negative relationship is being postulated between the level of supervision and organisational effectiveness.

Supervisory-Staff Ratio

Supervisory-staff ratio is an indicator of administrative intensity. This ratio is computed by dividing the total number of supervisors by total number on non-supervisory staff. Whereas the greater number of chains in the hierarchy may mean blockage of communication channels, conformity to roles and adverse effect on employee's performance and job satisfaction, the increase in supervisory-staff ratios may mean better supervision, coordination and work efficiency. It will thus have a positive relationship with effectiveness.

Van de Ven and Ferry (1980) have used this variable for studying the effectiveness of E.S. offices in the United States, and have found strong positive correlations between overall office performance and supervisory-staff ratios. The present study proposes to study the positive relationship between this variable and variables measuring effectiveness, particularly the performance of the group and job satisfaction.

Task Variables

Task variables refer to the system by which the tasks are defined, distributed and standardised. (March and Simon, 1958). In the present study, they include a clearly defined distribution of work, placement of employee according to his qualifications and experience, and formalisation of rules and work procedures. The different components are described below.

Reporting and Distribution of Work

Work responsibilities and the reporting systems, wherever clearly defined, go a long way in increasing the accountability of the employees and present to them a framework within which their abilities are to be assessed. The organisational policies of performance appraisal, training and reward distribution will become meaningful only when responsibilities of the employees are defined in unambiguous terms.

Placement

Proper placement of employee will mean making a fit between his abilities and work (Porter et al, 1975). According to Brown (1966) work may be thought of as the use of man's physical and mental abilities to achieve a goal, where a selection is the process of finding the proper man to fill an opening. Placement is finding a proper opening for utilising man's abilities.

Work Procedures

Work procedures refer to the rules and regulations required for discharging the work responsibilities. Formalisation refers to the extent to which they are defined and followed (Van de

Ven and Ferry, 1980). It also refers to the details and clarity of the rules established, to guide the incumbent in his work performance. Melcher (1976) states :

> "... Problems may be unsolvable if the people lack the knowledge of the way in which solution can be obtained ... on the other hand, problems may be of nature where by the solutions or procedures for arriving at solution are well-known and it is a simple matter of applying these skills" (p. 91-92).

Work specification has been found related to work group cohesiveness, job involvement, and satisfaction (Graen, 1976), (Locke, 1976), (Raven and Rietsema, 1957), (Steers, 1976), (Sayeed and Vishwanathan, 1983). The present study proposes that a well defined task structure will induce better performance, provide job satisfaction and users' satisfaction and lead to effective functioning. Data regarding the variables have been collected through question items in O.A.S.-Questionnaire.

Policy Variables

In addition to monetary benefits, the organisational policies for assessment and distribution of rewards like performance appraisal, promotions and training programmes constitute important resources at the disposal of an organisation which it may offer to its employee in exchange of skills and energies spent by him in meeting the expectation of the organisation (Porter et al., 1975). If the organisational reward distribution and performance appraisal system is fair and contingent upon work, it will motivate the employee to perform better.

Porter and Steers (1973) state that recent research on attachment and withdrawal shows that continued attachment is strongly and positively correlated to overall job satisfaction, which is influenced among other factors by the pay and promotional policies of the organisation. Kanungo (1979) emphasises the importance of reward distribution pattern in motivating the employees and states : (a) Reward should be contingent upon performance, (b) Employee should attach valence to it, (c) Concrete rather than abstract reward should be offered.

Concrete reward captures the individual faster and the behaviour response is immediate.

The present study attempts to assess the fairness of the reward distribution system, performance appraisal methods, promotion and training policies through the question items in the O.A.S.-Questionnaire. It is assumed that fair policies will have positive impact on employees job behaviour, performance, job satisfaction, the user's satisfaction and organisatinoal effectiveness. The assumption of a significant positive relationship between the policy variables and effectiveness is based on the studies by Mott (1972), Porter et al. (1975), Sayeed and Vishwanathan (1983).

Collection Variables—Size of Collection

The collection of library, generally, consists of books, periodicals, thesis, technical reports, micro-films etc. The varied sources of information need to be properly organised for quick retrieval of the document when demanded. However, the differences in nature, format, and usage of a library collection make the organisation of a larger library collection a difficult task requiring proper decision and control at the stage of acquisition and processing of material. Wheeler and Goldhor (1962) hold the view :

> "If a library has only 'good' books on a subject, only good books can be borrowed. But there is evidence to indicate that the readers don't distinguish to any significant degree between 'good' books and 'bad' ones, but borrow each according to their ratio in a library collection" (p. 479).

For rendering good service to its users it is better that a library possesses a smaller but lively and currently useful collection, rather than larger but less useful one. Normally, library's collection becomes large and unwieldy, as it is not kept up-to-date by regular weeding out process. A high accountability of the librarians for the documents procured and regular checks by the audit in Indian libraries hamper the adoption of weeding policies. The increase in the size of the library collection in our libraries, may adversely affect the retrieval of the documents and their servicing and thus may lead to reduced user's satisfaction and effectiveness.

Climate Variables

Organisational climate refers to the perceived characteristics in the work environment that results largely from the action taken by the organisation and subsequently affect employee's behaviour (Steers, 1977). Climate has been thought to interact with individual characteristics of the employee to determine his behaviour at work. The variables studied under this are :

1. Leadership Style
2. Communication
3. Decision-Making

Leadership Style

Leadership is essentially an influencing process. Tennenbaum et al. (1959) define leadership as 'interpersonal influence exercised in a situation and directed, through the communication process, towards the attainment of specialised goals. What a manager expects from his subordinates and the way he treats them largely determine their performance and career progress (Livingston, 1969). An effective leader has to be both task-oriented and human relations oriented (Blake and Mouton 1969). Famous Howthorne studies have shown that interpersonal relations accounted for productivity in a greater measure than the physical environment of the worker. It has been found that more employee-centered leadership styles are generally associated with positive job attitude and behaviour (Frederickson, 1966), (Friedlander and Marguiles, 1969).

Managers who provide their subordinates with more autonomy and identity contribute significantly to achievement oriented behaviour where members feel more responsible for the attainment or organisational and group objectives, and thus contribute to higher organisational effectiveness. (Lawler et al. 1974) (Litwin and Stringer, 1968), (Marrow et al., 1967). Research in the Indian set-up has established that a democratic leader has a better chance of success and encourages better group cohesiveness (Grewal, 1963), (Chatterjee and James, 1965). Organisational conflict when openly confronted by the members or resolved by the supervisors can be a source of creative problem solving, which results in improved performance (Kelley, 1970).

Communication

Communication patterns and processes represent the necessary vehicle by which employee activities become coordinated and directed towards the goals and objectives of the organisation (Steers, 1977). Important organisational processes like leadership, decision-making rely heavily on communication for their implementation, their success is largely determined by effectiveness of the communication system. Robert Mc-Mury (1965) states that for communication to be effective, it must be two ways, there has to be a feed back from downwards to ascertain the extent to which the message has been understood and accepted. Stressing the need for upward communication, he states that the levels of supervision may become the levels blocking communication rather than the centres of communication. Horizontal communication is also essential to have good administrative control. Studies by Indian authors like Bhakru (1963), Shintre (1967) have stressed the role of communication in organisational success.

Decision-Making

Decision-making is universally defined as choosing between alternatives (Luthans, 1972). The decision by the manager has to be timely, rational, acceptable and goal-oriented. The manager may have to make unique one time decisions like wage negotiation, extension of working hours, or routine types of decisions. There are many well defined techniques of decision-making avilable to a modern manager today, yet he may adopt any particular style of management depending upon the management value he subscribes to. (Luthans, 1972).

A major issue concerning managerial approaches to decision making is the extent to which managers allow their subordinate to participate in decisions affecting their jobs (Steers, 1977).

It has been, generally, found that more supportive and participative decision-making leads to increased job satisfaction, lower turnover and absenteeism, and increased cooperation among members (Filley and House, 1969), (Steers and Porter, 1974). Studies by Indian authors like Choudhury (1955), Grewal (1963), Malviya (1977), Jhuney (1976) report positive results of worker's participation on his job attitude, involvement, job satisfaction and performance.

The climate variables chosen for the study have been measured through question items in O.A.S.-Questionnaire. Based on the studies cited above a positive relationship between climate and organisational effectiveness is presumed.

Inter-Unit Coordination

A unit normally consists of a supervisor and all personnel reporting directly to that supervisor (Van de Ven and Ferry, 1980). Organisational unit may obstruct the achievement of corporate goals and strategies or alternatively support the overall purpose of the organisation (House, 1963). The tasks assigned to organisational unit represent cycle of activities that are organised to meet the ultimate goals of the organisation are highly interdependent. This is specifically true of library organisations. The related tasks, therefore, need to be grouped together and the process of coordination to manage their interdependence are to be clearly spelt out. The efficiency of well coordinated units will reflect the effective functioning of organisation.

In a modern library organisation coordination and integration of unit level activities is highly relevant and desirable. If quality and quantity of output at each stage is not controlled, standardized, and coordinated properly, the final output may be far below the standard. It will mean a loss of information to the users since it will become difficult to retrieve the proper document. Inter-Unit coordination provides a link between the structural, task, policy variables and employee behaviour, and so becomes an important intervening variable contributing to organisational effectiveness. Based on the studies cited above and the collective nature of work in library organisation, the present study, assumes that inter-unit coordination has a positive influence on the performance of the libraries. Data regarding this variable are obtained through the question items in the questionnaire.

Employee's Job Behaviour

Different employees possess different outlooks, goals, needs, and abilities. These human variations often cause people to behave differently from one another, even when placed in the same environment (Steers, 1977). It is the employee who contitutes organisational structure, makes use of technology and responds to climate. The key to organisational success lies in the manner in which the employee work together to ensure the ultimate success of the organisation. Employee's job design has thus become a central concern for management practitioners and others.

The initial expectations of writers like Taylor (1911) and Weber (1947) were that by simplifying, standardizing and specialising jobs, work could be done more effectively. Subsequent research showed that simple routine non-challenging jobs led to employee's dissatisfaction. The concept of job enlargement and expansion was introduced to overcome these difficulties (Argyris, 1957) (Harzberg, Hausner and Snyderman, 1959). Recently, studies by Turner and Lawrence (1965), Hackman and Lawler (1971), and Hackman and Oldham (1975) have tried to resolve the conflict between job simplification and job enlargement. Their findings establish that certain characteristics of individuals themselves must be taken into account along with job characteristics to arrive at a proper prediction of behaviour at work.

Job Characteristics, Background Characteristics and Job Affiliations

Turner and Lawrence (1965) conducted a study to find out the relationship between job characteristics and employees' reactions like job satisfaction and work attendance. A positive relationship between the two was observed in smaller towns, but the results did not fully support the assumption. Porter et al. (1975) stress the implications of workers' job design for organisational effectiveness and state that it has to be done by matching his background characteristics and job characteristics. To incorporate flexible job design to suit the requirement of the worker, organisational design has to be flexible.

Hackman and Oldham (1975) have studied the five core job dimensions through their 'Job diagnostic survey' which measures job attitudes of the workers on an eight point scale. The instrument represents a major conceptual and empirical contribution to the study of job design as it integrates earlier works on job design. It specifies the job characteristics that along with individual characteristics lead to positive or negative outcome at work places. Steers (1977) on the other hand, emphasises the need for growing the employees affiliation to the organisation so that organisations may attract and maintain a steady flow of qualified persons, make them engage in spontaneous and innovation behaviour, and secure dependable performance from them.

In this study, employee's job behaviour has been studied keeping in view the above approaches. Information is sought through question items on employee's job characteristics like autonomy, responsibility, initiative, standard of job, his background variables, and job affiliations. Based on the research cited above, the employee's job behaviour variable is presumed to have a positive influence on the effectiveness of the libraries.

Development of Hypotheses

A survey of the literature on organisational effectiveness and effectiveness of the library organisations has already been presented as a background to this study. On the basis of this, the factors measuring and influencing effectiveness have been identified. The rationare for choosing the factors and their proposed relationships to the field of present investigation have been discussed in detail under each factor in the foregoing analysis. Research evidence has been cited to justify the choice of factors and for building up the major hypothesis which are being examined in the study. The following hypotheses are framed :

Hypothesis I

(a) The size of the library organisation will be negatively related to effectiveness (Raven, 1959, Van de Ven and Ferry, 1980),

(b) The degree of specialisation will be negatively related to effectiveness (Child, 1973 ; Van de Ven and Ferry, 1980).

(c) The number of supervisory levels will be negatively related to effectiveness (Van de Ven and Ferry, 1980 ; Sunderarajan, 1984).

(d) The supervisory-staff ratio will be positively related to effectiveness (Van de Ven and Ferry, 1980).

Hypothesis II

The task variables (such as the distribution of work, placement of the employee and work procedures) will be positively related to effectiveness (Mott, 1972 ; Osburn and Hunt, 1974).

Hypothesis III

The policy variables (such as reward and punishment, performance appraisal, and training) will be positively related to effectiveness (Sayeed and Vishwanathan, 1983 ; Padaki, 1984 ; Sunderarajan, 1984).

Hypothesis IV

The collection variable will be negatively related to effectiveness.

Hypothesis V

The climate variables (like leadership style and communication) will be positively related to effectiveness. (Padaki, 1984 ; Sunderarajan, 1984)

Hypothesis VI

The inter-unit coordination variable will be positively related to effectiveness (Agrawal, 1975 ; Van de Ven and Ferry 1980).

Hypothesis VII

The employee's job characteristics will be positively retated to effectiveness (Hackman and Lawler, 197 ; Hackman and Oldham, 1975).

Hypothesis VII (a)

The employee's background variables will be related to employee's job behaviour variable. (Hackman and Lawler, 1971 ; Hackman and Oldham, 1975).

Hypothesis VIII

Effectiveness of library organisation can be measured by the variables like the employee's job satisfaction, performance of the group, user's satisfaction and the rate of growth (Van de Ven and Ferry, 1980 ; Cameron, 1981 ; Padaki, 1984 ; Sunderarajan, 1984).

Hypothesis IX

There will be a difference in effectiveness between the two types of organisations (Sunderarajan, 1984) i.e. the special and academic library organisations ;

Hypothesis IX(a)

Because of differences in relationship between the structural variables (size, degree of specialisation, supervisory levels, supervisory-staff ratios) and effectiveness variables.

Hypothesis IX (b)

Because of differences in relationship between the task, policy, climate, coordination, employee variables and effectiveness variables.

Hypothesis X

Factors accounting for differences in the most effective and the least effective organisations are the policy, task, climate and employee factors (Padaki, 1984 ; Sunderarajan, 1984).

Hypothesis XI

The variable measuring the user's satisfaction will be related to one another (Sahoo, 1979).

Hypothesis XI (a)

The user's background variables (like the age, sex, marital status, educational and professional qualifications, length of library membership and experience in service) will not be related to the user's satisfaction.

6

Development of Instruments

Efficient data collection requires that measurement devices be short, require minimum effort to be administered to a large number of people at a time and yet maintain acceptable standards of reliability and validity (Van de Ven and Ferry, 1980). From this point of view Questionnaires, and organisational records have been used to collect data. These were supplemented by the interviews of selected number of employees at the time of Pilot Study to find out if the instrument was properly understood and responded. Some senior employees of the organisations were also interviewed to get information about design, staff structure and the budget of the organisations. Instruments used in the study are depicted in Table 6.1.

TABLE 6.1

Instrument used in the Study

Variables	Instrument Used
Independent : Influencing Effectiveness	
1. Task, Policy, Coordination, Employee	Organisation Assessment Survey Questionnaire I and II
2. Structural, Collection	Organisational Record Profile
Measuring Effectiveness	
3. User's Satisfaction	User's satisfaction scale
4. Employee's Job Satisfaction	Job Satisfaction Scale
5. Group Performance	Group Performance Scale
6. Rate of Growth	Organisational Record Profile

Instruments Used for Measuring Independent Variables

Organisation Assessment Survey Questionnaire—'Appendix A'

Keeping in mind the model adopted for the study, a questionnaire, based on Van de Ven and Ferry's (1980) Organisational Assessment Instrument and Campbell and Beaty's (1971) dimensions of organisational climate, has been designed to measure factors influencing organisational effectiveness. This was a five point scale. The independent variables measured by the questionnaire were : (1) Task variables such as reporting and work distribution, work procedures and placement. (2) Policy variables like reward and punishment, performance appraisal and training. (3) Climate variables as leadership styles, communication and decision-making. (4) Coordinating variables. (5) Employee's job behaviour variables like job characteristics, his background and job affiliations.

Design of the Questionnaire

The questionnaire has been divided into two parts : Section 'A' and Section 'B'. Section 'A' records the general information regarding the background of the respondent which is collected through choice of Fixed Response Categories and Information Blanks. Section 'B' contains the questions measuring independent variables except structural and collection variables. An attempt has been made to use simple English sentences to obtain information as library employees at all levels of organisation (except the lowest, clerical, and technical ones) have been included in the survey. The response catgories have been standardised in simple terminology in the form of anchor points written over the five point scale so that the respondents may circle the appropriate response without much difficulty. Champaney (1941) and Guilford (1954) have stated that the cues provided should be clear, consistent, precise, objective and unique. Cues of very general nature like superior, poor, and having implications good or bad, desirable or undesirable have been avoided.

Logic Behind Five Point Scale

Guilford (1954) suggests that the number on a rating scale should be selected on the basis of several logical considerations. Van de Ven and Ferry (1980) state :

> "If too few scale points are used... much information is lost because the scale does not capture the discriminatory power, the respondents are capable or making. On the other hand, hy adding too many scale points, the scale can become graded so finely that it is beyond the respondent's limited power of discrimination" (p. 62).

Going by the opinions of these authors, a five point scale has been considered ideal for measuring the responses of the employees. The five point scale has been adopted uniformly even in other instruments used in the study.

Validity

The face validity of any instrument ultimately rests with the degree of consensus that can be obtained from heterogeneous groups of experts. The present questionnaire on organisation assessment survey was given to fifteen experts belonging to the field of teaching, practising administrators and professional librarians. Their qualitative comments and areas of disagreement and agreement were taken into consideration in finalising the questionnaire. Those items which showed a minimum of 70 per cent agreement among the experts were retained.

Pilot Study

The pilot study was conducted on twenty employees of an academic library using O.A.S.- (Appendix- 'A'). To further establish the validity and reliability of the instrument, interviews were conducted with the employees to determine whether the respondents interpreted the questionnaire items in the way that were intended. The ambiguous terms were modified, the implicit, repetitive or questions showing no relevance to the real work situation were dropped. Inter-item correlations for each item meant to measure a variable were examined. Item showing significant correlations with other items of a variable was retained. Item (Items) not showing significant correlation with other items of the same variable was/were dropped. A few questions on employee's sense of belonging of the organisation were added. The items dropped out of O.A.S.-I and the reasons for doing so is given in the Table 6.2.

Reliability of the Final Questionnaire

A new questionnaire incorporating the necessary changes has been used for final study (O.A.S.-Questionnaire-II, Appendix-'A'). Factor analysis using Varimax Method of Rotation has been done to form variables for final analysis. The reliability of this instrument by Odd and Even Method of reliability test has been found to be highly significant, (r=.634). (Appendix—'E')

Organisational Record Profile (Appendix—'E')

Vital organisational data regarding structural variables such as size of the library, degree of specialisation, supervisory levels, and supervisory-staff ratios and data about size of the library collection have been obtained from the records of organisation recorded through 'Organisational Record Profile' under six important headings : History, Collection, Budget, Staffing Pattern, Work Organisation and Membership. Information obtained through these items has been used to form the structural and collection variables.

TABLE 6.2

Question Items Retained and Dropped out of the Organisation Assessment Survey Questionnaire-I after the Pilot Study (N=20)

No.	Variable	Item Nos. retained	Item Nos. dropped	Remark		
1.	Reporting and work distribution	1,2,4	3	3 +1 3 +2	r=.322 r=.229	NS NS
2.	Coordination	5,6,8	7	7 +5 7 +6	r=.239 r—.177	NS NS
3.	Placement	9,10	None			—
4.	Work Procedure	11,12	None			—
5.	Reward and punishment	15,16	None			—
6.	Performance Appraisal	17,18	14 19	14+17 14+18	r=.064 r=.228	NS NS
7,	Training	20,21	None			
8.	Goal Congruence	—	22	Respondents found it implicit		
9.	Decision-making	23,24,29	None			—
10.	Communication	26,27,28	None	Terminology modified		

1	2	3	4
11. Leadership	30		
Styles	31,32,33	None	Terminology modified
12. Conflict resolution	34,35	None	
13. Employee Behaviour	13,36,37	35	35+37 r=.180 NS
	38		35+38 r=.380 NS
		39	39+37 r=.225 NS
			39+13 r=.364 NS
14. Job Attitude	None	41	Ambiguous and repetitive
15. Employee's job Satisfaction		40	Adopted as a separate scale

r=.444 significant at P<.05
r=.561 significant at P<.01
NS=Not significant

Size of the Organisation

The size of the organisation has been worked out on the basis of total number of employees working in the organisation. Table 6.3 depicts the size of the organisation as adopted for the study.

TABLE 6.3

Different Sizes of the Library Organisations

Staff strength of the Library	Size	Score Used
Below—20	Small	1
21—40	Medium	2
41—60	Large	3

Degree of Specialisation

This has been compiled from the number of sections recorded under the heading 'Work Organisation' in the Organisational Record Profile. The number of sections in which libraries were organised ranged between 1-6. The organisation of the libraries also differed on the basis of the functions of the libraries and nature of material obtained. A library may be divided into sections on the basis of material procured, e.g. books and journals, or according to functions performed such as, acquisition, processing, and servicing of documents of all kinds. Figure 4 and 5 display the most commonly observed division of work in libraries.

Supervisory Levels

Supervisory levels have been counted on the basis of different strata manifested in the reporting patterns of the organisations. Normally, two to three levels of supervisions have been observed, the range varied between 1-3. Supervisory levels have also been depicted in the figures 4 and 5.

Supervisory-Staff Ratio

Supervisory-staff ratios are indicative of the degree of administrative control. It is hypothesised that they have

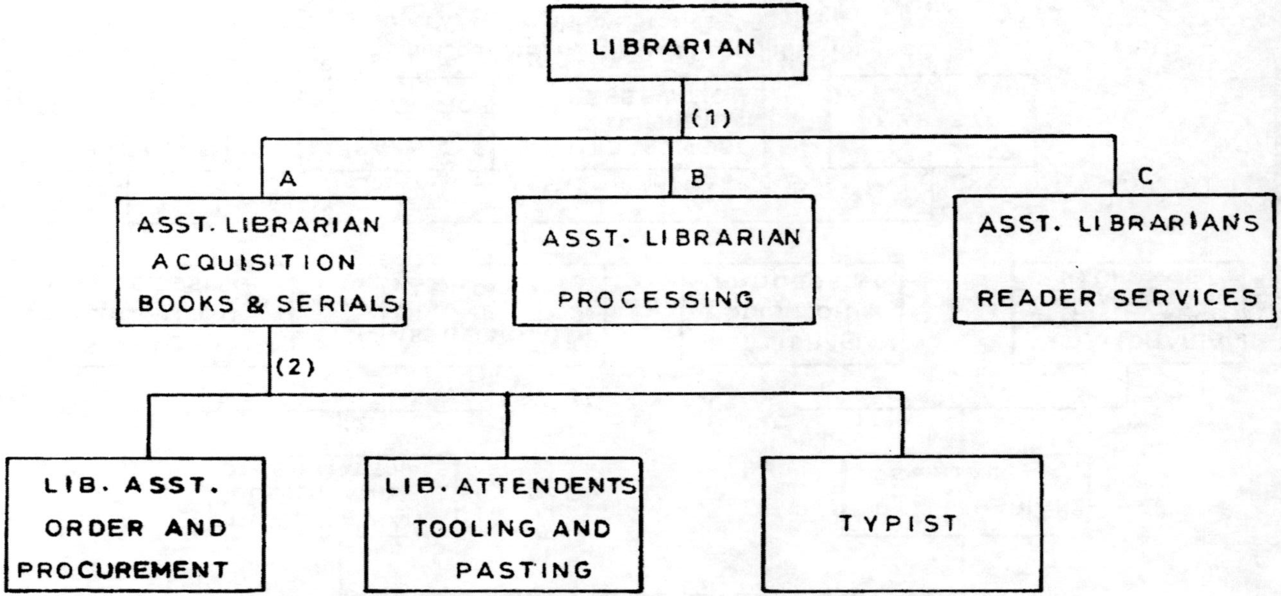

Fig. 4. Some specimen of degree of specialisation and supervisory levels in libraries.

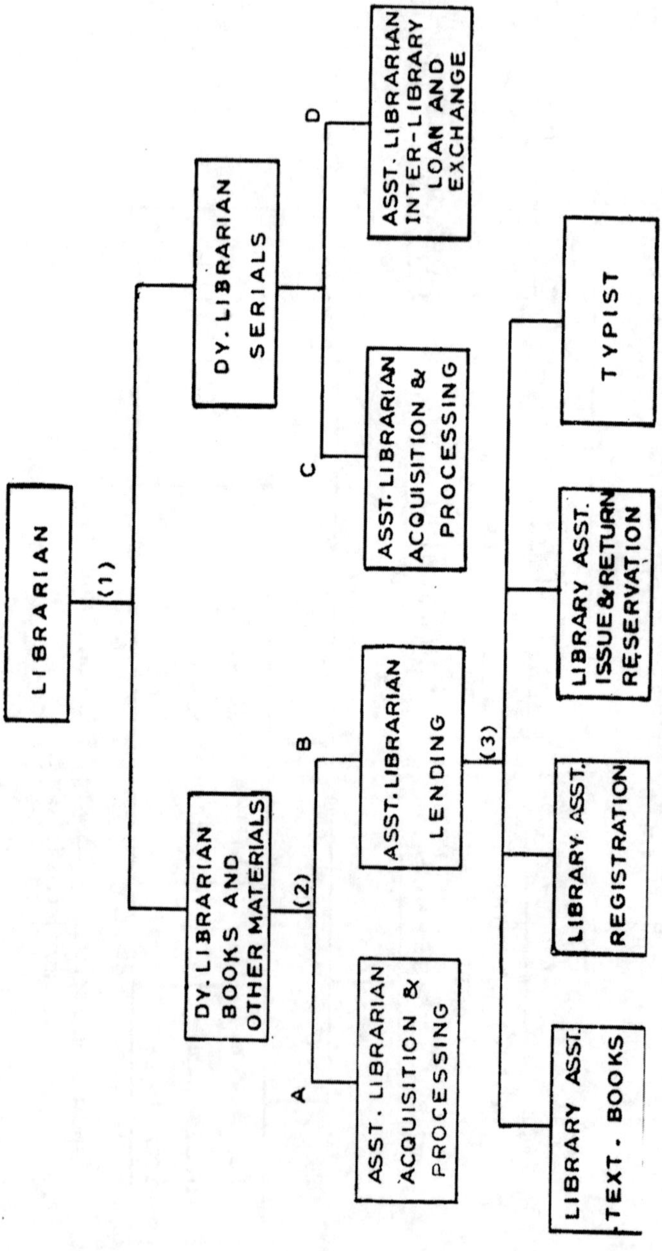

Some specimen of degree of specialisation and supervisory levels in libraries

significant positive relation with organisational effectiveness. The ratio has computed as total number of supervisors divided by total number of non-supervisory personnel in an organisation. The data obtained through organisational record profile have been used to work out the supervisory-staff ratio. For calculation purposes the fraction representing supervisory staff ratio is expressed in terms of decimal unit.

Collection Variable

The strength of the total collection of the library comprisng the books, journals, reports, conference proceedings and other special materials as obtained through organisation record profile has been used to work out the size of the library. Table 6.4 depicts the size of the library collection as adopted in the present study.

TABLE 6.4

Different Sizes of Library Collection

Collection	Categorization	Score used
Upto 50,00	Small	1
50,000 to 100,000	Medium	2
Above 100,000	Large	3

Instruments Used for Measuring Organisational Effectiveness

User's Satisfaction Scale—Appendix-'B'

In the present study, the questionnaire 'on user's satisfaction is based on a recent study named 'User's Survey Concerning Teachers and Research Scholars using I.I.T. Delhi Library' by Sahoo (1978). All important dimensions along which users satisfaction was measured in this questionnaire have been retained, but the responses have been collected on a five point scale and response cues have been provided. In this respect, the instrument used is an improvisation of the existing one.

Section A of the questionnaire is designed to collect information about the background of the users such as age, sex, marital status, discipline, status, educational qualification, experience in the service and length of library membership. Section-B contains questions on user's satisfaction relating to important functions of the library. The eight dimensions of library functioning covered are :

1. Library collection and its upto-dateness.
2. Efficiency of procurement of material.
3. Library records.
4. Sources of information.
5. Arrangement on shelves.
6. Services provided by the library.
7. Assistance from library staff.
8. Satisfaction with the timings of the library.

The researcher, based on her own long experience of working in the library, felt satisfied with the choice of the dimensions selected for judging the user's satisfaction. To further strengthen the choice, a small survey seeking the opinions of the users regarding 'user's satisfaction dimensions', was conducted, the result of the survey confirmed the choice. To obtain unbiased opinions of the users, the researcher personally visited the reading halls of the libraries on certain specified days and handed over the questionnaires to them. An attempt was made to seek opinions from different categories of users and from those who had atleast three years of association with the library. The satisfaction index for a user has been derived by summing up his opinion on all the eight dimensions. In the final study, mean scores of user's satisfaction scale for each library have been worked out and are given in Table 6.5.

Validity and Reliability

The content validity of the questionnaires was established by adopting the items from a previous study as well as by the opinion survey of the users. The test re-test reliability of the measure on 10 per cent of the population after three months interval was found to be quite high ($r=0.63$).

TABLE 6.5

Total and Mean Score of User's Satisfaction for the Libraries N=15

Code for the Libraries	No. of Respondents	Total Score	Mean Score
Special Libraries			
01	7	371	53.40
02	7	400	57.00
03	10	637	63.70
04	10	616	61.10
05	7	461	65.85
06	13	649	49.92
07	12	786	65.50
08	11	649	59.00
Academic Libraries			
09	18	1105	61.38
10	22	1141	51.86
11	16	837	52.31
12	21	1195	56.90
13	18	1136	63.11
14	17	892	52.47
15	10	568	56.80

Employee's Job Satisfaction Scale (Appendix-'C')

The job satisfaction scale used for the present study was adopted from Van de Ven and Ferry (1980) who used a modified version of job staisfaction index used in 'Survey of Organisation (Taylor and Bowers, 1972)'. The instrument measures on a five point scale where response categories vary between very unsatisfied to very satisfied, employee's job satisfaction alongwith six important dimensions such as : (1) Job, (2) Supervisor, (3) Co-worker, (4) Pay, (5) Career progress made and (6) Career progress in future. Employees were asked to express their opinions on the above dimensions. The employee's job satisfaction index was obtained by adding his responses on the six items. However, to reduce the data to organisational level, mean scores of job satisfaction for each library have been used for the final analysis and are given in Table 6.5.

TABLE 6.6
Total and Mean Score of Employce's Job Satisfaction in the Libraries N=15

Code for the Libraries	No. of Respondents	Total Score	Mean Score
Special Libraries			
01	16	261	16.31
02	13	168	12.92
03	8	180	22.50
04	7	145	20.71
05	10	273	27.30
06	9	148	16.44
07	16	260	16.25
08	11	229	20.81
Academic Libraries			
09	12	275	22.91
10	26	434	16.69
11	10	186	18.60
12	10	252	25.20
13	24	537	22.37
14	18	268	14.88
15	13	279	21.46

Validity and Reliability

The result of the studies by Van de Ven and Ferry (1980) showed the questionnaire items were quite effective in measuring the job satisfaction. Thus all the items in the questionnaire had content validity. The test-re-test validity of the instrument on 10 per cent of the population after three months of interval was quite high (r=0.65 on an average).

Group Performance Scale (Appendix-'D')

The group performance scale used in this study is adopted from Performance Evaluation Form, Vyasulu (1984) who used it as a measure of Supervisor's performance. The performance of the group has been rated on five point scale. The five response categories described the performance as very low, low, average, high and very high. Six important dimensions of performance measured were : (1) Work performance, (2) Job knowledge of team members, (3) Initiative taken in discharging responsibilities, (4) Cooperation among the team members, (5) Reliability of the group as a whole, (6) Leadership traits among the team members. The supervisors in each library were asked in confidence to rate the group working under them. Since the norm of internal assessment in library organisation is of similar nature, there was no problem faced by the researcher in getting the performance rating of the group by the supervisors. Mean scores for group performance for each library were obtained and used for final study and are given in Table 6.7.

TABLE 6.7

Total and Mean Score of Group Performance in the Libraries N=15

Code for the Library	No. of Respondents (Supervisors)	Total Score	Mean Score
Special Libraries			
01	2	33	16.50
02	2	27	13.50
03	2	46	23.00
04	2	43	21.50
05	2	52	26.00
06	2	30	15.00
07	2	42	21.00
08	2	45	22.50
Academic Libraries			
09	2	46	23.00
10	2	32	16.00
11	2	32	16.00
12	2	51	26.50
13	2	48	24.00
14	2	31	15.50
15	2	47	23.50

TABLE 6.8

Budget Figures and the Percentage Increase Over Previous Years for the Libraries N=15

(Budget in Rupees)

Code for the Libraries	1980-81	1981-82	1982-83	1983-84	Percentage increase
Special Libraries					
01		120,000	130,722	156,000	15.00
02		480,000	480,000	480,000	00.00
03	274,348	347,439	392,898		21.60
04		100,000	100,000	125,000	12.50
*05		600,000	704,000	785,000	29.33
06			5,092,000	6,074,000	19.28
07		400,000	580,000	625,000	28.12
08		1,800,000	2,000,000	2,300,000	13.88
Academic Libraries					
09		700,000	700,000	900,000	14.28
10		1,900,000	2,100,000	2,700,000	15.78
11		760,000	800,000	860,000	06.57
12		238,000	266,000	356,000	37.80
13		400,000	650,000	875,000	59.00
14		2,750,000	3,075,000	3,300,000	10.00
15		300,000	360,000	400,000	17.00

*Figures include value of journals received in exchange.

Rate of Growth Index

This index has been compiled from the data obtained regarding the budgets of the organisation for the previous three year (i.e. 1980-81, 1981-82 and 1982-83) as the comparable figures for longer periods were not available for all the libraries under study. The rate of increase in the budget has been calculated over the previous two years and is expressed as a percentage. This percentage as expressed correct upto four significant digits, has been adopted as one of the indices of effectiveness in the final study and is given in Table 6.8.

7

Methodology

Libraries situated in Delhi was the universe for the purpose of this study. The library organisations can broadly be classified into three types namely ; academic, special, and public. Whereas academic and special libraries have a firm footing in the network of libraries in our country, the concept of free universal public library service has yet to take roots in India. Besides, the objectives of academic and special libraries can be somewhat similarly, defined, the needs of their users can be identified and their organisational pattern can be studied under a comparative reference. As Simsova (1982) states :

> "In comparative studies, a researcher will most likely be motivated by intellectual curiosity, the object of which will not be the description of an event, but rather some theoretical issues underlying it" (p. 10).

The public libraries, on the other hand, have very wide objectives of supplementing the formal education helping people good citizens (Bhattacharjee, 1979) ; their clientele may range from literate to neo-literate, even the blind making use of these libraries by having access to Braille facilities. They may have a loose network of many branch libraries. Since one of the objective of the present study was to determine the factors that account for differences in the effectiveness of different type of libraries, the academic and special libraries where such comparison might be feasible, have been chosen for study. A brief description of each type is given below.

Special Libraries

A clear, distinct and generally acceptable definition of a special library has not yet developed, although many writers have presented their definitions, since the beginning of the century (Kent, 1980). Special libraries have, generally, been defined in following ways :

(a) A library having special subject collection e.g. a law library.

(b) A library having special subject collection and/or collection in special format e.g. a Museum library which may have separate collections of micro-films, microfisches and photographs.

(c) A library having special collection organised for use by a specialised clientele e.g. Defence Services library.

The first definition concentrates on the nature of collection, the second on the format, and the third on the needs of the clientele. In practice, special libraries may and can exist at any of the above levels and satisfy the needs of their parent entities (Kent, 1980).

One major misunderstanding about specialised libraries is that each library may be concerned with a special subject alone. Normally, this is not a true picture. A library may specialise in one major area and have collection on allied subjects e.g. a library on Archaeology may also have books on sculpture, history, and religion besides archaeology. In the present study, the special libraries are chosen to correspond to the above categorisation of such libraries.

Academic Libraries

Academic libraries can be defined as the libraries attached to the institutions of learning with a specific object of lending support to their curricula and other related activities. In institutions of higher learning and universities, these libraries add another dimension to their objectives, viz., supporting the research and consultancy work being carried in the parent bodies.

The idea of establishing universities in India was conceived in 1854, and three major universities of Bombay, Calcutta and Madras were established by 1857. As no teaching functions were assigned to the universities, apparently, no need was felt for the establishment of the libraries. The libraries thus sprang later, the university libraries in Bombay and Calcutta were established in 1864, and in Madras in 1873. The real progress, however, came after Independence after the adoption of the five year plans. In India, at present, there are 120 universities, 15 institutions deemed to be universities, and 10 institutions of national importance (Gupta, 1985).

The present day university library system comprises the central library, broad-based subject libraries such as law, science and social libraries, and campus libraries. These libraries are completely independent in matters of finance, library, committees, and selection procedures and policies. Their link with the parent body is of a routine administrative nature. In the present study, the academic libraries chosen are the ones belonging to institutions of higher learning, institutions of national importance, and institutions deemed as universities. The school and college libraries have been excluded from the perview of the academic libraries as they are relatively small organisations and present little diversity.

Special vs Academic Libraries

Special libraries differ from academic libraries in respect of their clientele and nature of collection. As Blagden (1980) states :

"Special libraries are special because they serve a restricted clientele, who work in an organisation with comparatively specific goals" (p. 28).

The users of special libraries make up homogeneous groups having more or less defined needs. The nature of collection is also restricted to a broad area and its allied fields. There may, thus, be a cohesive library-user relationship in these organisations. The users of the academic libraries may be undergraduate and postgradute students, research scholars and teachers who academic needs may vary from textbooks, research material to specialised technical reports, and conference proceedings. The clientele of these libraries is large and demanding. Their collections also consist of diverse subjects and material. The compact library-users relationship may be missing in such a set-up.

Sample

In the present study, sampling has been done at different levels. In the first level, seven academic and eight special libraries have been drawn on the basis of purposive sampling (reasons discussed in detail earlier).

Stratified random sampling has been done in choosing the respondents from amongst these libraries so that employees at all levels might be covered. It has been amply demonstrated in previous researches that the perception of a few managers are not generalisable to the functioning of the entire organisation (Dearborn and Simon, 1958 ; Porter, 1958). On the assumption that the most knowledgeable informants of the pattern of structure and processes within the organisation are the people who work at different levels, it has been decided to adopt the stratified random technique so that when their perceptions are aggregated in a specific way, we may get a reliable measure of organisational behaviour which is closer to reality. Professional and semi-professional library staff upto the level of library attendants have been included for sampling. Clerical and office staff have been excluded.

Simple random sampling on a certain number of days has been done to choose the respondents from amongst the library users whose opinions have been obtained to evaluate the libraries.

Size

203 employees and 200 users of the fifteen academic and special libraries formed the sample of the survey. 203 employees working at different levels of these organisations have provided information through organisation assessment survey questionnaire-II for measuring independent variables (except structural variables). Job satisfaction of the same 203 employees has been measured through a job satisfaction scale. 200 users of these libraries formed the sample for measuring user's satisfaction.

Features

Most of the libraries covered in this study were attached to a parent body and had an assured source of finance. The policies of the parent organisations applied to the libraries also. However, a few of the libraries were attached to privately registered organisations and did not have set policies or enhanced budgets. Though most of the libraries provided lending facilities, a few permitted only consultation. The oldest among the libraries was established in 1902 and the youngest in 1982. The sample covered libraries belonging to universities, government departments, autonomous bodies and privately registered bodies. Prominent features of the sample are depicted in Table 7.1. .

Data Collection, Processing and Analysis

The data have been collected from 203 employees and 200 users of the library organisations selected for the study by means of separate instruments over a period of six months. The questionnaire on Organisational Assessment Survey was handed over to the libraries and their objective opinions were obtained assuring them of the secrecy of their responses. The opinions of the employees were also recorded in confidence against the items, whenever desired. The organisational data were obtained from annual reports, special reports and also by interviewing the senior members of the staff. Data regarding

TABLE 7.1

Prominent Features of the Sample Under Study

Code	Type	Parent Body	Year of Establishment	Size	No. of Sections	Supervisory Levels	Size of Collection
1	2	3	4	5	6	7	8
01	Special	Government	1902	Medium	4	2	Medium
02	,,	Registered Body	1943	Medium	6	1	Large
03	,,	Government	1965	Small	3	2	Small
04	,,	Registered Body	1956	Small	3	1	Small
05	,,	Government	1935	Small	2	2	Small
06	,,	Government	1926	Large	5	3	Large
07	,,	Autonomous	1964	Medium	4	2	Medium
08	,,	Government	1952	Medium	2	1	Large
09	Academic	Autonomous	1956	Medium	1	1	Medium
10	,,	,,	1961	Large	5	2	Large
11	,,	University	1969	Small	3	2	Medium
12	,,	,,	1924	Small	3	2	Medium
13	,,	,,	1949	Medium	3	2	Large
14	,,	,,	1982	Small	4	2	Medium
15	,,	,,	1973	Small	4	2	Medium

performance of the groups were obtained from the supervisors who were requested to rate, in confidence, the performance of the group (groups) working under them.

Data from the users were obtained by making a direct contact with them. The researcher visited the reading halls of each library and personally handed over the questionnaire (on user's satisfaction) to the users in order to obtain their unbiased opinions regarding their libraries. In some special libraries where usual attendance was very thin, the researcher visited the library regularly for a week and, at times, sought the help of the library staff, to collect the completed questionnaires. Even then, in some of the special libraries, the responses collected remained small.

Processing and Analysis of Data

Independent Variables

The data collected from employees and users of the libraries were coded, punched and verified for computerisation. The data collected from employees with the help of organisation assessement survey questionnaire-II to measure variables influencing organisational effectiveness (such as work distribution, placement and procedure ; training, performance appraisal, reward and punishment, inter-unit coordination, decision making, leadership, communication and employee variables) were factor-analysed.

Factor Analysis

Factor analysis is commonly used for selecting the best items within each scale and later a theoretical meaning is assigned to the scale (Van de Ven and Ferry, 1980). Varimax method of matrix rotation was used to select the factors for final study. The items with .5 values were selected to form a factor. Table 7.2 shows the factor loading, for each item, factors formed, their Eigenvalues and percentage of variance. Five factors with Eigenvalues nearing one were selected. Screen test was applied to the curve plotting the Eigenvalue as displayed in Figure 6. Interestingly, the factors emerging after the factor loading more or less matched with the design of the

TABLE 7.2

Factor Analysis for 36 Items in Organisation Assessment Survey Questionnaire-II by Varimax Method. Eigenvalues and Cummulative Percentage of Variance

Item No.	Policy Factor	Coordinating Factor	Employee Factor	Task Factor	Climate Factor
1.	.253	.774	.159	—.195	—.253
2.	.322	.726	.153	—.214	—.205
3.	.250	.766	.153	—.209	—.245
4.	.203	.793	.210	—.184	—.167
5.	.214	.756	.216	—.267	—.267
6.	.224	.689	.321	—.253	—.223
7.	.044	.257	.228	—.792	—.182
8.	.041	.264	.259	—.810	—.165
9.	.343	.318	.195	—.557	—.299
10.	.296	.380	.080	—.492	—.271
11.	.754	.231	.160	—.087	—.264
12.	.747	.267	.196	—.057	—.227
13.	.632	.254	.136	—.173	—.339
14.	.814	.208	.109	—.107	—.131
15.	.495	.478	.274	—.058	—.351
16.	.296	.197	.339	—.116	—.315
17.	.679	.138	.250	—.227	—.315
18.	.720	.209	.219	—.228	—.326

1	2	3	4	5	6
19.	.655	.228	.184	—.064	—.374
20.	.351	.378	.279	—.247	—.575
21.	.333	.342	.303	—.213	—.595
22.	.343	.498	.230	—.063	—.532
23.	.392	.156	.163	—.240	—.689
24.	.347	.190	.163	—.323	—.661
25.	.316	.170	.172	—.186	—.603
26.	.158	.311	.153	—.286	—.706
27.	.460	.248	.252	—.271	—.598
28.	.423	.196	.313	—.338	—.576
29.	.459	.231	.389	—.027	—.557
30.	.369	.315	.524	—.094	—.430
31.	.325	.286	.546	—.211	—.229
32.	.230	.195	.778	—.303	—.125
33.	.136	.206	.639	—240	—.335
34.	.083	.104	.812	—.163	—.135
35.	.466	.335	.557	—.004	—.391
36.	.450	.376	.482	—.021	—.454
Eigenvalues	19.459	2.226	1.647	1.366	.989
% of Cummulative Variance	54.045	60.230	64.807	68.603	71.351

Significant loading of items on a factor= .50

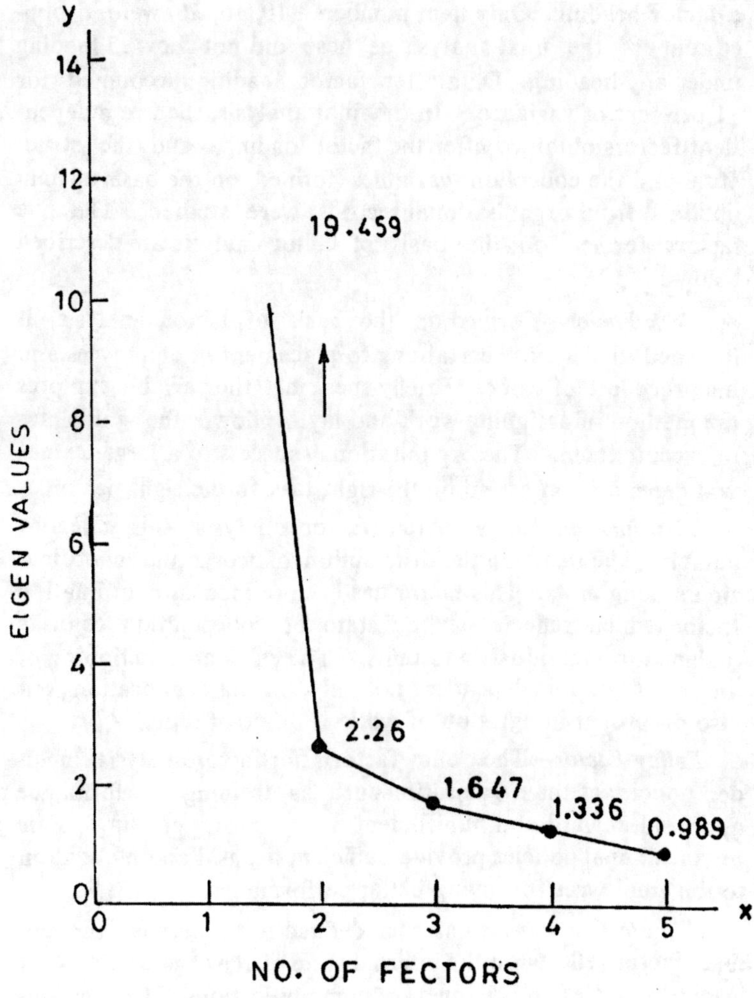

FIG. 6 Eigenvalues of five independent factors obtained after analysis

study given in Chapter 4 with minor adjustment of items under a factor heading. Only item numbered 10, 16, 36 were dropped out of the final analysis as these did not show .5 loading under any heading. Data after factor loading accounted for 71 per cent of variance. In the final analysis, the five independent factors obtained after the factor loading, and the structural and the collection variables (formed on the basis of data obtained from organisational records) were studied. The five factors formed on the basis of factor analysis are described below :

Task Factor—Formed on the basis of factor analysis, it included the items pertaining to placement of employees and his procedure of work. Briefly speaking, the variable explores the method of assigning work and laying down the guidelines to execute them. The organisational success to a large extent will depend upon assigning the right task to the right person.

Coordination Factor—After factor analysis, this category combines the items on the distribution of work and coordination among units. This factor has been termed as coordination factor which reflects on the state of coordination of tasks assigned to individuals and units. The efficient functioning of an organisation is dependent not only on task allocation but also on proper integration of work at different units.

Policy Factor—The policy factor after factor analysis included policies of the organisation such as training, performance appraisal, reward and punishment and decision-making. Fair organisational policies provide sufficient arousal and motivation to the employees for giving better performance.

Climate Factor—As has been defined in the study, the climate factor reflects on the internal state of the organisation—its leadership styles and channels of communications. The decision-making styles of the leader, however, formed part of the policy factor, after the factor analysis.

Employee Factor—This factor included items on job characteristics, and job affiliation of the employees which ultimately reflect his job behaviour.

Reducing Data to Macro-Organisational Level

The data regarding the structural variables such as size, number of sections, supervisory levels and supervisory staff ratios compiled from organisational records were available at the organisational level or macro-level. But the data which were obtained through the perceptions of employees and users remained at the micro-level. To make it comparable with other types of data, it had to be reduced to the macro-organisational level. To achieve this purpose, the mean score of each factor was worked out separately for different libraries on the basis of the items combined under each factor after factor analysis. Thus, the data pertaining to all independent variables were reduced to organisational level and made comparable.

Variables Measuring Effectiveness

The data pertaining to variables measuring effectiveness have been collected from four different sources through different instruments discussed in detail in Chapter 4. Table 7.3 lists the instruments used scales, scores dimensions, sources of information and number of respondents. A brief discussion about the computation of these variables for final study is given here.

Reducing Data to Macro-Organisational Level

Mean scores were computed for the data collected from fifteen special and academic libraries through 'Employee's Job Satisfaction Scale', 'User's Satisfaction Scale' and 'Group Performance Scale'. This was done to reduce the data to the Macro-organisational level and to make it comparable with other data. The data pertaining to the budget was taken from organisational records. The percentage increase in the budget over the previous two year's budget, provided the score for growth index. The Mean Score for User's Employees, Group performance variables, and the score for Growth Index formed the data for measuring effectiveness of the libraries chosen for study. Table 7.4 depicts the data pertaining to independent variables and variables measuring effectiveness after processes as used in the final analysis.

Inter-item correlation analysis between the data pertaining to independent variables and criteria variables (all reduced to organisational level) was done to study the hypotheses formed.

TABLE 7.3

Scales, Scores, Sources of Information and number of Respondents for Variables Measuring Effectiveness Total Sample (N=15)

No.	Instrument	Dimension	Scale	Score	Sources of information	No. of respondents/year
1.	User's Sati faction Scale	8	5 pt.	80	User's of the Library	200
2.	Employee's Job Satisfaction Scale	6	5 pt.	30	Employee's of Library	203
3.	Group Performance	6	5 pt.	30	Supervisors	30
4.	Rate of Growth	Budget 1980-81, 1981-82, 1982-83	Figures	Percentage increase per year	Organisational records	3 yrs.

TABLE 7.4

Processed Data Pertaining to Variables Influencing Effectiveness and Variables Measuring it as Used in the Final Analysis (N=15)

Code of the Library	Variables Influencing Effectiveness						
	Size of collection	Size of organisation	Degree of specialisation	Supervisory levels	Supervisory staff-ratio	Coordinating	Policy
	1	2	3	4	5	6	7
01	2	2	4	2	00.13	18.12	15.00
02	3	2	6	1	00.05	14.92	10.69
03	1	1	3	2	00.20	25.00	29.50
04	1	1	3	1	00.20	16.28	21.86
05	1	1	2	2	00.20	26.20	31.50
06	3	3	5	3	00.10	18.55	15.88
07	2	2	4	2	00.13	20.69	16.50
08	3	2	2	1	00 08	27.09	23.54
09	2	2	1	1	00.08	26.08	28.33
10	3	3	5	2	00.12	15.77	13.85
11	2	1	3	2	00.17	20.04	23.70
12	2	1	3	2	00.20	24.10	28.10
13	3	2	3	2	00.12	23.92	24.29
14	2	1	4	2	00.20	15.28	15.50
15	2	1	4	2	00.25	26.38	26.07

	Variables Measuring Effectiveness						
Code of the Library	Task	Climate	Employee	Rate of Growth	User's Satis-faction	Employees Satisfaction	Group Perfor-mance
1	8	9	10	11	12	13	14
01	09.44	22.38	19.31	15.00	53.00	16.31	16.50
02	11.38	27.15	15.00	00.00	57.00	12.92	13.50
03	11.87	41.12	26.75	21.60	63.00	22.50	23 00
04	11.00	34.28	22.14	12.50	61.00	20.71	21.50
05	12.90	45.80	27.80	29.33	65.85	27.30	26.00
06	09.55	25.88	18.33	19.28	49.92	16.44	15.00
07	11.81	26.44	20.06	28.12	65.50	16.25	21.00
08	12.54	37.54	22.82	13.88	59.00	20.81	22.50
09	11.33	38.25	23.33	14.28	61.38	22.91	23.00
10	07.96	23.27	17.42	15.78	51.86	16.69	16.00
11	09.70	31.10	20.10	06.57	52.31	18.60	16.00
12	11.30	42.40	25.20	37.80	56.90	25.20	25.00
13	11.00	37.30	24.04	59.00	63.11	22.37	24.00
14	17.11	21.72	18.00	10.00	52.47	14.88	15.50
15	11.38	39.76	23.46	17.00	56.80	21.46	23.50

Note : Data for column No. 1—5 obtained from Organisational Records
Data for column No. 6—10 obtained from the employee
Data for column No. 11—14 obtained from different sources explained in Table 7.3.

8

Results and Discussion

To achieve the major objectives of the study, the hypotheses as presented in Chapter 5 were framed. The results are discussed here with a view to determining the extent to which they agree with the hypotheses.

Mean, standard deviation, and inter-correlation analysis using 'Product Moment-Coefficient of Correlation' were computed for different sets of data to test the hypotheses framed. Fisher's 't' tests were also computed to find out the significant differences between the functioning of the academic and the special libraries, and the least effective and the most effective group of libraries. The following different sets of data were analysed.

(i) Total sample (N=15) to study hypothesis I to VIII (except VII (a).

(ii) Comparative study of special (N=8) and academic (N=7) libraries to study hypothesis IX.

(iii) Comparative study of the most effective (N=5) and the least effective (N=5) libraries, chosen on the basis of effectiveness indicies, to explore hypothesis X.

(iv) User's background variables, user's satisfaction index and library dimensions (N=200 users) to study hypothesis XI-XI (a).

(v) Employee's background variables and his job behaviour variables (N=203 employees). The result of inter-correlation analysis between the two were used to study hypothesis VII (a).

Hypothesis I

(a) The size of the library organisation will be negatively related to effectiveness (Raven, 1959 ; Van de Ven and Ferry, 1980).

(b) The degree of specialisation will be negatively related to effectiveness (Child, 1973 ; Van de Ven and Ferry, 1980).

(c) The number of supervisory levels will be negatively related to effectiveness (Van de Ven and Ferry, 1980: Sunderarajan, 1984).

(d) The Supervisory-staff ratio will be positively related to effectivenes (Van de Ven and Ferry, 1980).

The inter-correlation matrix displaying relationship among structural variables and criteria variables for total number of libraries (N=15) is presented in Table 8.1. The results obtained indicate the following :

Size of the Organisation

The size of the organisation displays no significant relationship with effectiveness as the obtained correlation values are below the level of significance. Hypothesis 1 (a) is not supported by the result.

Degree of Specialisation

The degree of specialisation as reflected by the number of sections bears negative relationship with the three criteria

TALBE 8.1

Inter-correlations between Structural Variables and criteria Variables in Libraries (N=15)

Structural Variables	Rate of Growth	User's Satisfac tion	Employee's Job Satisfaction	Group Performance
Size of the Organisation	.002	—.318	—.462	—.441
Degree of Specialisation (Number of Sections)	—.275	—.532*	—.779**	—.735**
Supervisory Levels	.345	—.357	—.058	—.154
Supervisory-Staff-Ratio	.150	.095	.437	.403

* Significant at $p < .05$ level of significance

** Significant at $p < .01$ level of significance

variables, reflecting negative impact of task interdependence on the functioning of the organisation (Melcher, 1976). A significant negative relationship ($p < .05$) is displayed with the user's satisfaction and a highly significant negative relationship ($p < .01$) is shown with job satisfaction and group performance. The results obtained also find support in the study of Child (1973) who reported negative relationship between the specialisation and organisational effectiveness. Hypothesis 1(b) is supported by the results.

Supervisory Levels

The supervisory levels display no significant relationship with effectiveness. Significant relationship did not emerge, perhaps, due to the fact that libraries under survey did not reflect much variation in the level of supervision. Hypothesis 1(c) is not supported by the result.

Supervisory-staff Ratios

The Supervisory-staff ratios do not display any significant

relationship with effectiveness as the computed values are below the level of significance. The hypothesis 1(d) gets no support from the result.

Hypothesis II

The task variables (such as the distribution of work, placement of employee, and work procedures) wlll be positively related to organisational effectiveness (Mott, 1972; Osburn and Hunt, 1974).

The task variable after the factor analysis consisted of the items pertaining to the placement of the employee and work procedures. Table 8.2 displays the relationship of this variable with criteria variables.

TABLE 8.2

Correlation Coefficients (r) between Task Factor snd Criteria Variables in Libraries (N=15)

Variables Measuring Effectiveness	r
User's Satisfaction	.784**
Job Satisfaction	.603*
Group Performance	.712**
Rate of Growth	.274 NS

* Significant at $p < .05$ level of significance
** Significant at $p < .01$ level of significance

The task factor displays significant positive relationships with the employee's job satisfaction, user's satisfaction and group performance variables. The relationship between the growth variable and the task variable is insignificant. From the significant positive relationship of the task variable with three of the criteria variables, it can be deduced that the task variable contributes significantly to organisational effectiveness. The result of the study finds support in the studies that have reported positive relationship between role clarity (work specificity) and increased goal commitment, work group cohesiveness and employee's satisfaction (Graen, 1976 ; Raven

Reietsema, 1957 ; Steers, 1976 ; Sayeed and Vishwanathan, 1983). The above discussion and the result lend support to hypothesis II.

Hypothesis III

The policy variables (like reward and punishment, performance appraisal and training) will be positively related to organisational effectiveness (Sayeed and Vishwanathan, 1983 ; Padaki, 1984 ; Sunderarajan, 1984).

The policy factor after factor analysis consisted of the items pertaining to reward and punishment, training, performance appraisal and decision-making. Table 8.3 displays the relationship between the policy factor and the criteria variables.

TALBE 8.3

Correlation Coefficients (r) between Policy Factor and Criteria Variables in Libraries (N=15)

Variable Measuring Effectiveness	r
User's Satisfaction	.550*
Employee's Job Satisfaction	.950**
Group Performance	.866**
Rate of Growth	.412 NS

** Significant at p<.01 level of significance
* Significant at p<.05 level of significance

The policy factor displays a positive and highly significant (P<.01) relationship with job satisfaction and performance variables. Its positive relationship with the user's satisfaction is shown by r=550 (P<.05). Only the relationship with the rate of growth variable (r=.412) is statistically insignificant. From the above it can be concluded that the policy factor is significantly related to organisational performance. Such results find support in the studies of Mott, 1972 ; Porter et al., 1975 ; Sayeed and Vishwanathan, 1983. The result and discussion support hypothesis III.

Hypothesis IV

The collection variable (reflecting the size of the library collection) will be negatively related to effectiveness.

The values of correlation coefficients between collection variable and the measures of effectiveness is presented in Table 8.4.

TABLE 8.4

Correlation Coefficients (r) between Collection Variable and Measures of Effectiveness (N=15)

Measures of Effectiveness	r
Rate of Growth	.030 NS
User's Satisfaction	—.457 NS
Employee's Job Satisfaction	—.488 NS
Group Performance	—.451 NS

NS=not significant

The discussion on the correlates of effectiveness' in Chapter 3 gives a rationale for assuming a negative relationship between the size of the library collection reflecting the volume or material to be handled and library effectiveness. The obtained correlations between the two are, however, not significant. This may be due to small size of the sample. The results do not lend support to hypothesis IV.

Hypothesis V

The climate variables (like leadership style and communication) will be positively related to organisational effectiveness (Padaki, 1984 ; Sunderarajan, 1984).

The climate variable after factor analysis consisted of the items relating to leadership styles and communication. Table 8.4 given below shows relationship between climate, factor and criteria variables.

The climate factor displays a significant positive ($p<.01$) relationship with the job satisfaction and group performance

TABLE 8.5

Correlation Coefficients (r) between Climate Factor and Criteria Variables in Libraries (N=15)

Variables Measuring Effectiveness	r
User's Satisfaction	.630*
Employee's Job Satisfaction	.932**
Group Performance	.889**
Rate of Growth	.425 NS

*Significant at $p < .05$ level of significance.
**Significant at $p < .01$ level of significance.

variables. The relationship with the user's satisfaction is at $P < .05$ level of significance ($r = .630$). The relationship with the rate of growth variable is statistically insignificant. The positive climate factor representing conducive working conditions has been found to be associated with positive job attitude and behaviour (Frederickson, 1966 ; Friedlander and Marguiles, 1969) and thus with performance and job satisfaction (Steers, 1977).

The positive organisational climate also indicates free and open channels of communication which contribute to organisational success by coordinating and directing employees activities towards organisational goals (Bakhru, 1963 ; Shintre, 1967 ; Steers, 1976). The positive relationship of the climate variables with effectiveness shown in the study finds support in the literature quoted above. The results and studies quoted above support hypothesis V.

Hypothesis VI

The inter-unit-coordination variable will be positively related to organisational effectiveness (Agrawal, 1975 ; Van de Ven and Ferry, 1980).

The coordination factor after factor analysis consisted of the items pertaining to distribution of work and inter-unit coordination. Table 8.6 shows the relationship of the coordinating factor with effectiveness variables.

TAALE 8.6

Correlation Coefficients (r) between Coordination Factor Criteria Variables in Libraries (N=15)

Variables Measuring Effectiveness	r
User's Satisfaction	.547*
Employee's Job Satisfaction	.805**
Group Performance	.840**
Rate of Growth	.447 NS

**Significant at $p < .01$ level of significance
*Significant at $p < .05$ level of significance.

The coordination factor displays a positive and significant ($p < 01$) relationship with job satisfaction and group performance variables ($r = .805$ and $r = .840$ respectively). The relationship shown with the user's satisfaction is at $p < .05$ level of significance ($r = .547$). However, its relationship with the rate of growth variable is not statistically significant. The coordination factor shows positive significant relationship with three criteria variables. The result of the study finds support in the work of Shull, Delbecq and Cummings (1970) and Agrawal (1975). The positive coordination policies facilitate the task of the employees, induce positive job behaviour, better performance, job satisfaction, user's satisfaction and effectiveness. The result and discussion above lend support to hypothesis VI.

Hypothesis VII

The employee's job characteristics variables will be positively related to effectiveness (Hackman and Lawler, 1971 ; Hackman and Oldham, 1975).

Table 8.7 displays the relationship between the employees job factor and the criteria variables.

The employee factor displays a positive significant ($P < .05$) relationship with the growth variables and a positive and highly significant ($P < .01$) relationship with all other variables.

TABLE 8.7

Correlation Coefficients(r) between Employees Factor and Criteria Variables in Libraries (N=15)

Variables Measuring Effetiveness	r
User's satisfaction	.658**
Employee's job satisfaction	.954**
Group Performance	.932*°
Rate of Growth	.556*

* Significant at $P < .05$ level of significance
**Significant at $P < .01$ level of significance

The positive significant relationship of this factor with all the measures of effectiveness highlights its primary role in the functioning of an organisation. The importance of the employees' job characteristics in relation to effectiveness is emphasised in the work of Porter et al (1975) Pierce (1978), Hall et al (1977) and Steers (1977). The results of the study and the literature cited above lend full support to hypothesis VI.

Hypothesis VII (a)

The employee's background variables will be positively related to the employee's job behaviour variable (Hackman and Lawler, 1971 Hackman and Oldham, 1975).

The data regarding the background of the employee's were collected through O.A.S. Questionnaire-II (Section-A). The relationship of the background variables with the employee's job behaviour variables (for 203 respondents) has been worked out separately and presented in Table 8.8. The implications of this relationship have been used to discuss hypothesis-VI (a).

The results indicate that employee's job behaviour bears a positive relationship with his educational qualifications and designation. The relationship with educational qualifications ($r=.181$) is highly significant at $p< .01$ level of significance. The correlation values obtained for other variables are not statistically significant. The study does not establish a relationship between professional qualifications and job behaviour variable. This may be due to the fact that a large number of employee in the libraries are promoted on the basis of their length of service rather than on achieving higher professional qualifications. The relationship between educational qualifications and higher designation and the employee's job behaviour is reasonable and logical.

TABLE 8.8

Correlation Coefficients(r) between Employee's Background Variables and Employee's Job Behaviour in Library Organisations (N=203 Employees)

Background Variables	r
Age	.016
Sex	.101
Marital Status	.056
Educational Qualification	.181**
Professional Qualification	.099
Experience	.011
Designation	.161*
Nature of Work	—.086

* Significant at P <.05 level of significance
**Significant at P <.01 level of significance

The role of the employee's background characteristics and job characteristics in determining the employee's performance has been emphasised by Nemiroff and Ford (1976), Hackman (1976) and Porter et al. (1975). They in fact, suggest a three way fit between the workgroup, job design, and the individuals background for achieving a high level of job satisfaction and performance. This study has established the positive significant relationship between only two of the background variables and employee's job behaviour. The results of the study lend partial support to hypothesis VII (a).

Hypothesis VIII

The effectiveness of a library organisation can be measured in terms of four sets of criteria variables : the employee's job satisfaction, group performance, user's satisfaction and the rate of growth variables.

Table 8.9 displays a relationship between the independent variables and criteria variables and present the following picture :

Employee's Job Satisfaction

This factor displays a highly significant negative relationship with the degree of specialisation variable, highly significant and positive relationships with the coordination, policy, climate and employee factors and a significant positive relationship with the task variable.

Group Performance

The factor displays a highly significant negative relationship with the degree of specialization and a highly significant positive relationships with the task, coordination, policy, climate and employee factors.

User's Satisfaction

This factor displays a significant negative relationship with the degree of specialization, a highly significant positive relationship with the employee and task factors and a significant positive relationship with the coordination, policy and climate factors.

Rate of Growth

This factor is positively related to the employee factor (r= .556). It does not reflect any significant relationship with other independent variables. The insignificant relationships of this variable with other independent variables may be due to the fact that it consisted of only budget figures. However, the growth of a library organisation may be constituted by many other factors like an increase in the lending transactions, reference queries answered, membership enrolement etc. These

TABLE 8.9

Inter-correlations between Correlates and Criteria Variables in Library Organisations (N=15)

Independent Variables	Growth Rate	User's Satisfaction	Employee's Job Satisfaction	Group Performance
1. *Structural*				
(i) Size of the Organisation	.002	—.318	—.462	—.441
(ii) Degree of Specialisation	—.275	—.532*	—.779**	—.735**
(iii) Supervisory Level	.345	—.357	—.058	—.154
(iv) Supervisory Staff-Ratio	.150	.095	.434	.403
2. *Collection* Size	.030	—.457	—.488	—.451
3. *Coordination*	.447	.547*	.805**	.849**
4. *Task*	.274	.784**	.603*	.712**
5. *Policy*	.412	.550*	.950**	.866**
6. *Climate*	.425	.630*	.932**	.889**
7. *Employee*	.566*	.658**	.954	.932

**Significant at P $\leq$.01 level of significance

*Significant at P $<$.05 level of significance.

factors could not form part of this study due to the lack of data in this field.

The results thus indicate that three of the four criteria variables are influenced, though in varying degrees, by most of the independent variables. The rate of growth variable, however, reflects a weak and insignificant relationship with most of the independent variables (except the employee variable). It can, therefore, be stated that excepting the rate of growth variable, all other measures are indicative of effectiveness in library organisations. The result and discussion above thus lend partial support to hypothesis VIII.

Hypothesis IX

There will be a difference in effectiveness between two types of organisations (Sunderarajan, 1984) i.e. the special and academic library organisations :

(a) Because of differences in relationship between the structural variables (size, degree of specialisation, supervisory levels, supervisory staff ratios) and effectiveness variables.

(b) Because of differences in relationship between the task, policy, climate, coordination, employee variables and effectiveness variables.

Hypothesis IX (a)

Inter-correlation analysis between the structural variables and criteria variable for academic (N=7) and special libraries (N=8) are presented in Table 8.10.

ACADEMIC LIBRARIES

Size of the Organisation

The positive or negative relationship shown by the size of the organisation variable with criteria variables are statistically insignificant.

Degree of Specialisation

The negative relationships borne by degree of specialisation to criteria variables are statistically insignificant.

TABLE 8.10

Correlation Coefficients of Structural and Collection Variables and Criteria Variables in Special and Academic Libraries

Independent Variables	Academic Libraries (N=7) Criteria V				Special Libraries (N=8) Criteria V			
	Rate of Growth	User's Satis-faction	Employee's Job Satis-faction	Group perfor-fance	Rate of Growth	User's satis-faction	Employee's Job Satis-faction	Group Perfor-mance
Structural								
Size of the Library	0.148	0.121	—0.146	—0.132	—0.197	—0.753*	—0.698	—0.726*
Degree of Specialisation	—0.112	—0.663	—0.602	—0.485	—0.525	—0.565	—0.883**	—0.925**
Supervisory Levels	0.203	—0.485	—0.312	—0.261	0.596	—0.302	0.014	—0.127
Supervisory-Staff-Ratios	—0.163	—0.391	0.062	0.030	0.591	0.560	0.752*	0.715*
Collection								
Size	0.526	0.163	—0.143	—0.067	—0.495	0.645	—0.688	—0.688

**Significant at p <.01 level of significance
* Significant at p <.05 level of significance

Supervisory Levels

It displays a negative but statistically insignificant relationship with the three measures of effectiveness. Thc positive relationship with the rate of growth variable is also statistically insignificant.

Supervisory Staff-Ratios

This variable displays statistically insignificant relationship with all the measures of effectiveness.

The results of the study indicate that the structural variables reflecting the size, degree of specialisation, pattern of hierarchy, and supervisory staff-ratios do not display any significant relationship with the functioning of an academic library set-up. The results thus point out that reasons for the better functioning of academic libraries may have to be found beyond their structural design.

SPECIAL LIBRARIES

Size of the Organisation

The size of the library is significantly and negatively related to two measures of effectiveness. It thus bears a significant negative relationship with organisational effectiveness.

Degree of Specialisation

This variable shows significant negative $(P<.01)$ relationships with job satisfaction and group performance variables. Being significantly related to two measures, it greatly influences organisational effectiveness.

Level of Supervision

This variable does not display any significant relationship with any of the measures of effectiveness.

Supervisory Staff-Ratio

The variable displays significant positive $(p<.05)$ relationships with job satisfaction and group performance variables, thus supporting the view that increased administrative staff-ratios will lead to better performance.

None of the structural variables discussed above has shown any significant relationship with any measure of effectiveness in academic libraries, whereas all of them, except supervisory levels, have shown a positive or negative relationship with at least two of the measures of effectiveness in special libraries. The result of the study thus supports hypothesis IX(a).

Hypothesis IX (b)

Inter-correlation matrix between the coordination, task, policy, employee and climate variables and criteria variables for academic (N=7) and special libraries (N=8) is presented in Table 8.11.

Academic Libraries

(i) All factors, except the policy factor, display a positive and highly significant ($p<.01$) relationship with employee's job satisfaction and group performance varibles. The relationship of policy factor is significant at $p<.05$ level (with group performance variable).

(ii) The coordination and employee factors display a positive and significant ($p<.05$) relationship with user's satisfaction variable also.

(iii) None of the factors displays a significant relationship with the rate of growth variable.

Special Libraries

Coordination Factor

This variable is showing a significant positive ($p<.05$) relationship with two variables only viz., job satisfaction and group performance.

Task Factor

The task variable shows a positive and highly significant relationship with user's satisfaction, and a positive and significant relationship with group performance variable. The significant relationships are with two variables only.

TABLE 8.11

Correlation Cofficients of other Independent Variable and Criteria Variables in Academic and Special Libraries

Independent Variables	Academic Libraries(N=7) Variables Measuring Effectiveness				Special Libraries (N=8) Variables Measuring effectiveness			
	Rate of Growth	User's satis-faction	Employee's job Satisfac-tion	Group perfor-mance	Rare of Growth	User's Satis-faction	Employees Job Satis-faction	Group perfor mance
1. Coordination	.385	.778*	.892*	.902**	.599	.487	.750*	.786*
2. Task	.462	.735	.941**	.902**	.284	.837**	.606	.751*
3. Policy	.327	.673	.937**	.822*	.586	.612	.973**	.912**
4. Climate	.493	.711	.968**	.933**	.376	.656	.920**	.851**
5. Employee	.618	.790*	966**	.965**	.658	.644	.962**	.931**

**Significant at p $\lessdot$.01 level of significance

Policy Factor

The policy variable displays a highly significant ($p<.01$ level) relationship with job satisfaction and group performance variables. Again the relationship is significant in terms of two variables.

Climate Factor

The climate factor shows a highly significant ($P<.01$) relationship with employee's job satisfaction and group performance variables. No significant relationship is shown with the rate of growth and user's satisfaction.

Employee Factor

This variable also displays a positive and highly significant relationship with two variables, viz., group performance and employee's job satisfaction. No significant relationship is shown in terms of user's satisfaction and the rate of growth.

In special libraries the following picture emerges :

(i) All factors display significant relationship with two variables only.

(ii) All factors, except the task factor, display positive and significant relationship with group performance and employee's job satisfaction, though the level of significance varies.

(iii) The task factor shows very significant ($r=.837$) relationship with user's satisfaction variable.

(iv) The relationship of these factors with the rate of growth variable is statistically significant.

Comparing these results with that of the academic libraries, the following differences in two sets of libraries are observed :

(i) In the academic libraries, all factors (except policy) display a positive and highly significant relationship with group, performance, and employee's job satisfaction variables whereas in the special libraries the task factor does not display any significant relationship with these two variables.

(ii) Whereas in the academic libraries coordination and employee factors display positive relationships with the user's satisfaction, in the special libraries only task factor shows positive relationship with user's satisfaction variable.

Though the above cited differences in the role of task, coordination, policy, climate, and employee factors vis-a-vis effectiveness factors were observed in the special and academic libraries, a clear cut picture to support or reject the hypothesis did not emerge. To further test the hypothesis, 'Fishers' 't' Test of A difference between Means was applied to these factors.

Table 8.12 displays the mean differences, standard deviations and 't' ratios between the academic and special libraries for policy, climate, employee, task and coordination factors.

The result of 't' statistical analysis clearly reveals that there are no significant differences in the mean values of these factors in the two types of libraries. Therefore, 't' ratios are also not significant. The insignificant 't' ratios of coordinating, policy, task, climate, and employee variables is academic and special libraries are 0.305, 0.610, 1.575, 0.264, and 0.059 respectively. On the basis of insignificant differences in the means and insignificant 't' ratio, it can be concluded that the role of these factors does not substantially differ in academic and special libraries.

The results obtained on the basis of correlation analysis reflected the role of task, coordinating, policy, climate, employee factcrs in terms of only four variables which had been adopted as measures of effectiveness. In practice, many more measures of effectiveness may be there, which may give different picture vis-a-vis these factors. The results of 't' analysis clearly suggest that on an average the role played by these factors does not vary in academic and special libraries.

The result and discussion above indicate no support for hypothesis IX (b).

Hypothesis X

Factors accounting for differences in the most effective and the least effective organisations are the policy, task

TABLE 8.12

Mean, Standard Deviations, 't' Ratios of Coordinating, Task, Policy, Climate and Employee Factors in Special and Academic Libraries (N=15)

Variable	Organisation	N	Mean	SD	DF	't' Ratios	Level of Significance
Coordinating	Academic	7	21.653	4.670	13	0.305	NS
	Special	8	20.856	4.684			
Policy	Academic	7	22.834	5.856	13	0.610	NS
	Special	8	20.599	7.337			
Task	Academic	7	9.969	1.777	13	1.575	NS
	Special	8	11.311	1.270			
Climate	Academic	7	33.400	8.210	13	0.264	NS
	Special	8	32.574	8.377			
Employee	Academic	7	21.650	3.109	13	0.059	NS
	Special	8	21.526	4.285			

climate and employee factors (Padaki, 1984 ; Sunderarajan, 1984).

Separate intercorrelation analysis between the coordination, task, policy, climate, and employee factors of the five most effective and five least effective libraries (since the sample consisted of 15 libraries) has been done. The collection and structural variables have been excluded from this analysis as only one of them i.e. degree of specialisation displayed significant relationship with organisational effectiveness in the total sample (N=15). Table 8.13 displays the comparative picture.

Most Effective System

The relationships obtained are : (1) The task factor shows a positive significant correlation with the policy factor (r=.905). (2) The employee factor displays a positive significant relationship with the policy factor (r=.935). (3) The climate factor displays a positive significant relationship with the policy factor (r=.936). (4) The policy factor displays a positive significant relationship with task, climate and employee factors, (r=.905, r--.936 and r=.935 respectively). (5) The policy factor by virtue of its positive significant relationship with three of the five factors studied, emerges out to be a very significant factor distinguishing the most effective systems from the least effective systems.

Least Effective System

This state of affair is not observed in the least effective systems. The relationships displayed are generally weak and insignificant. In fact, none of the factors studied displays a significant positive relationship with the other factors in the least effective systems.

The result shown above lend support to hypothesis X. To find further support for the hypothesis, 'Fishers, 't' test of a difference between Mean's was applied to policy, climate, task and employee factors which emerged as distinguishing factors between the least and the most effective systems.

Table 8.14 displays the mean differences, standard deviations

TABLE 8.13

Intercorrelation between Coordinating, Task, Policy, Climate and Employee Factors in Five Most Effective and Five Least Effective Group of Libraries

	Most Effective N=5					Least Effective N=5				
	Coordination	Task	Policy	Climate	Employee	Coordination	Task	Policy	Climate	Employee
Coordination	1	.621	.426	.458	.219	1	.070	.812	.503	.835
Task		1	.905*	.874	.873		1	—.249	.582	—.442
Policy			1	.936*	.935*			1	.546	.837
Climate				1	.818				1	.092
Employee					1					1

*Significant at p <.05 level of significance.

TABLE 8.14

Mean, Standard Deviations, 't' Ratios of Policy Climate, Employee and Task Factors in Five Most Effective and Five Least Effective Group of Libraries (N=15)

Variable	System	N	Mean	Standard Deviation	DF	't' Ratio	Level of Significance
Policy	Most effective	5	27.892	2.825	8	4.269	$p < .01$
	Least effective	5	16.154	4.707			
Climate	Most effective	5	41.276	3.156	8	6.30	$p < .001$
	Least effective	5	25.646	3.81			
Employee	Most effective	5	25.45	1.81	8	6.10	$p < .001$
	Least effective	5	18.15	1.94			
Task	Most effective	5	11.690	.745	8	2.654	$p < .05$
	Least effective	5	9.436	1.525			

and 't' ratios for policy, climate, task and employee factors in the most effective and least effective set of libraries.

Significant differences are observed in the mean values of these factors in the two sets of libraries. The mean differences and 't' ratios derived indicated significant differences in the most and the least effective groups of libraries. These are depicted in Figure 7. The 't' ratios are very significant ($p<.001$) for the climate and employee factors, very significant ($p<.01$) for the policy factor, and significant ($p<.05$) for the task factor. The results of the 't' test fully support the earlier results derived on the basis of correlation analysis in these two groups of libraries. The results find support in the researches reported by Padaki (1984) and Sunderarajan (1984). The above results and discussion lend full support to hypothesis X.

Hypothesis XI

The variables measuring the user's satisfaction will be related to one another (Sahoo, 1979).

Table 8.15 displays the intercorrelations among eight variables chosen to measure the user's satisfaction in library organisations. Data obtained from 200 library users have been used for this purpose. The range and highest correlation shown by each variable with other variables are discussed.

Variables	Range of Correlation with other variables	Highest Correlation with variable name
1. Collection	.128 to .447	.447 processing
2. Efficiency of procurement and processing	.124 to .472	.472 records
3. Records	.187 to .496	.496 services
4. Sources of information	.005 to .525	.525 services
5. Arrangement on shelves	.218 to .517	.517 services

TABLE 8.15

Intercorrelation Matrix Showing Relationship between Eight Library Dimensions (N=200 Users)

Variables	1	2	3	4	5	6	7	8
1. Collection	1	.447	.405	.355	.344	.390	.354	.128
2. Processing and Procurement		1	.472	.329	.337	.459	.451	.124
3. Records			1	.343	.450	.496	.397	.187
4. Sources of Information				1	.414	.525	.403	.005
5. Arrangement on shelves					1	.517	.397	.218
6. Services						1	.550	.154
7. Assistance from staff							1	.193
8. Timings								1

r=.138 significant at $p < .05$ level of significance
r=.181 significant at $< .01$ level of significance

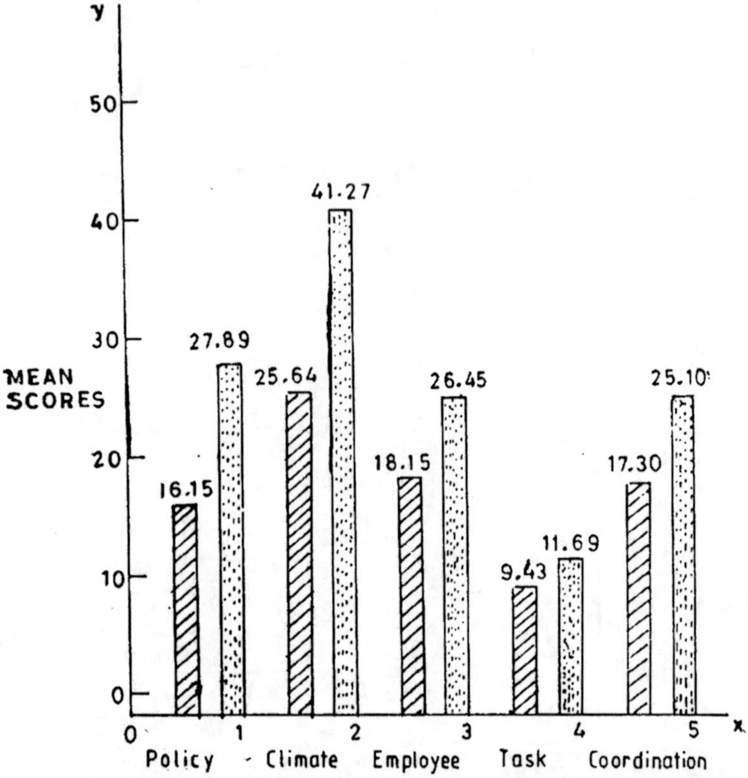

FIG. 7 Significant mean differences between the most and the least effective group of libraries

6. Services	.154 to .550	.550 assistance from staff
7. Assistance from staff	.193 to .550	.550 services
8. Library timing	.005 to .218	.218 arrangement on shelves

The results indicate the following positive and high correlations: collection and processing r=.447, processing and records r=.472, records and services r=.496, sources of information and service r=.525, shelf arrangement and service r=.517, staff assistance and services r=.550. These positive and significant relationships among different user's satisfaction variables lend support to hypothesis XI.

Hypothesis XI (a)

User's background variables (like age, sex, marital status, educational and professional qualifications, length of library membership and experience in service) will not be related with the user's satisfaction.

Table 8.16 displays the relationships between background factor and user's satisfaction index.

TABLE 8.16

Coefficient of Correlation (r) between User's Background Variables and User's Satisfaction Index in Library Organisation (N=200 users)

User's Background Variables	r
1. Age	.154*
2. Sex	.112
3. Marital Status	—.079
4. Discipline	—.161*
5. Status (Faculty/Undergraduate/Research/Postgraduate (others)	—.022
6. M.A./M.Sc./Ph.D.	.004
7. Length in Service (Experience)	.147*
8. Length of Membership of the Library	.088

* r=.138 significant at P <.05 level of significance

** r=.181 significant at P <.01 level of significance.

The role of background factors in influencing the user's satisfaction has not been a matter of investigation in the literature so far, therefore, the hypothesis had been framed on a non-relationship basis. The data about the user's background variables were collected through Section A of user's satisfaction questionnaire to investigate into this new field.

The results of the study indicate the following :

(i) The variables like sex, marital status, status, educational qualification and length of membership, show no relationship with user's satisfaction Index. ($r=.112$, $r=-.079$, $r=-.022$, $r=.004$ and $r=.088$ respectively).

(ii) Age shows a positive and significant relationship with the user's satisfaction, $r=.154$, ($p<.05$).

(iii) Experience in service shows a positive and significant relationship with the user's satisfaction, $r=.147$ ($p<.05$).

(iv) Discipline displays a significant negative ($r=-.161$, $p<.05$) relationship with the user's satisfaction. The disciplines coded on the higher side of the scale were the engineering and medicine. This reveals a significant trend which may be indicative of dissatisfaction of such professional groups with some of the libraries in their field and needs further investigation.

The results at (ii) to (iv) are contrary to the assumption of no relationship between the user's background variables and user's satisfaction variables. The results obtained, thus, do not fully support hypothesis XI (a).

9

Prominent Findings, and Summary

In this Chapter, the findings of the study are presented in accordance with the hypotheses developed under Chapter 5 and discussed under results in Chapter 8. Briefly stated, the broad set of hypotheses were :

The factors contributing to organisational effectiveness in library organisations are the structural factors (such as the size of the organisation, degree of specialisation, supervisory staff-ratios, and supervisory levels), the collection variable, and the task, policy, inter-unit coordination, climate and employee factors.

There will be differences in the effectiveness of the two types of organisations, i.e. the academic and special library organisations.

Significant differences in the most effective and the least effective organisations are in terms of the policy, task, employee, and climate factors.

The library effectiveness can be measured by criteria variables like the user's satisfaction, employee's job satisfaction, group performance, and the rate of growth of the organisation.

The user's satisfaction variables are related to one another and the user's background factors such as age, sex, experience in service will not influence that he derives from library use.

Now, regarding the first hypothesis, the study has established the significant negative relationship between the degree of specialisation and organisational effectiveness. Such results find support in the existing literature (Child, 1973 ; Van de Ven and Ferry, 1980). The assumed negative relationships of the size of the organisation, supervisory levels, and size of collection and the positive relationship of the supervisory staff-ratios with organisational effectiveness could not be supported by the results.

The result of the study has established the significant positive relationship between the task, coordination, policy, climate, and employee variables and effectiveness variables in library organisations. By highlighting the positive role of these factors, the study advocates the need for organising the libraries along the modern scientific principles of management to make them more effective and viable. Though libraries are not profit making organisation, their functioning needs to be reviewed, periodically, in view of the heavy public investment made in them.

Regarding the assumption of differences in effectiveness of two types of libraries. the study establishes the structural variables as being the distinguishing factors having influence on the effectiveness of special libraries. The special libraries, generally, may have a compact set-up and a small to medium size. The degree of specialisation and levels of supervisions are also few. The increase in size and degree of specialisation may disturb their equilibrium and have an adverse impact on their effectiveness. The results of the study have practical implications for special libraries and emphasise the need for structural design that will be conducive to their effective functioning. It may truly be said for special libraries that simple rules of organisational structure, if followed, can achieve results out of proportion (Nand, 1968). The results of the study further establish that the role of the task, policy, climate, employees and coordination variables does not significantly differ in special and academic libraries.

The results of the study have supported the hypothesis of significant differences between the most effective and the least effective libraries in terms of some independent factors. The significant differences in the mean values and 't' ratios of task, policy, climate, employee factors in the most effective and the least effective systems have revealed that their roles differ significantly in the two systems. As such, the effectiveness of libraries may not differ so much among the different types of libraries as between the most and the least effective libraries.

The study has attempted to measure the effectiveness of library organisations by criteria variables like the user's satisfaction, the employee's job satisfaction, group performance and the rate of growth. The results have established that three of the four criteria variables studied are influenced, though in varying degrees, by most of the independent variables. The employee's job satisfaction, group performance and user's satisfaction variables are indicative of effectiveness of library organisations.

The study has also investigated into the background factors of the employees that may possibly influence his behaviour at work. The results of the study indicate that employee's educational qualifications and designation bear a significant positive relationship with his job behaviour. The study, however, does not establish a relationship between the professional qualifications and the employee's behaviour at work in the libraries. An absence of such a relationship may be due to the fact that a large number of employees, at least at the lower cadres, get promoted on the basis of length of service rather than the achievement of higher professional qualifications.

The last, but not the least, important assumption made in the study was that user's satisfaction variables are related to one another. This assumption is greatly supported by the results of the study. The results of the study have also revealed that the age and experience of the user's have an influence on the satisfaction drawn from library use. The results also indicate that the users belonging to professional groups such as engineering and medicine have expressed negative views about the libraries. This may be an area for further investigation.

The Summary

To sum up the prominent findings are :

Increase in the degree of specialisation is negatively associated with *effectiveness of libraries.*

The structural variables like the size of the organisation and supervisory staff-ratios have a role in the functioning of *special libraries.*

Variables like the task, coordination, policy, climate, and employee (reflecting the proper allocation and integration of work, fair organisational policies, employee-oriented climate, and his positive job behaviour) will play a positive role in the functioning of the libraries *irrespective of the type to which the library belongs.*

The role of the policy, task, climate and employee variables differ significantly *between the least and the most effective libraries*

The effectiveness of a library organisation can be measured by criteria variables like the employee's job satisfaction, group performance and user's satisfactlon.

The rate of increase in the budget of a library organisation may not be taken as an index of its effective function.

In library organisations, the employee's background variables such as the age and educational qualifications have a significant relationship with his job behaviour.

No significant relationship has been found between the employee's professional qualifications and his job behaviour.

The user's satisfaction variables are related to one another.

User's background factors such as his age and experience have an influence on the user's satisfaction.

The users belonging to the professional groups like medicine and engineering have expressed lesser satisfaction with the functioning of their libraries, in comparison with the users belonging to the art, law and science groups.

The users of the libraries under survey, have expressed greater satisfaction with the services and staff assistance variables and lesser satisfaction with the timings of the libraries.

Implications

Some of the hypothesis examined in the study are supported by the results and important factors measuring and influencing effectiveness of the library organisations have been identified. The study, though not a final word on the design of the library systems, is definitely indicative of certain trends. It has implications for the design of special libraries, where variation in the size, degree of specialisation and supervisory-staff-ratios are likely to influence effectiveness.

Important implications of the study having bearing on the policy planning of the libraries are the following :

(a) The results of the study have indicated that an increase in the library budget is not a reliable index of its effective functioning. As such a mere increase in the budget allocations of a library may not be sufficient for improving its functioning.

(b) The study has indicated that the libraries differ in their functioning and that the most and the least effective libraries can be identified on the basis of their performance.

This highlights the scope for the Organisational Development (O.D) interventions in the library organisations in India after proper diagnosis of the problem in the concerned organisation (Saha, 1987).

(c) The users of the libraries under survey have expressed a low degree of satisfaction with the library timings. This suggests the need for reviewing the library timings, from time to time, based on the users opinions and demand (Saha, 1979).

(d) The users have expressed a high degree of satisfaction

with the services and staff assistance variables which indicate the users priorities and provide guidelines for reorganising the libraries wherever need arises.

(e) In some of the libraries, the professional groups of the users, such as the engineers and doctors have expressed lesser satisfaction with the functioning of their libraries which draws the librarian's attention towards improving the functioning of these libraries. Such opinions can not be simply ignored.

10

Some Observations and Suggestion

This study on the effective functioning of libraries in India was the first of its own kind to be conducted in the field. Designing the study at macro-organisational level involved lot of research, study and discussions at every stage. It was felt that evaluating libraries, by one simple parameter like user's satisfaction would do little justice to the complex concept of effectiveness. At the same time, it was not thought appropriate to form one compound index out of four heterogenous factors chosen to measure effectiveness, even though that would have made the computation and presentation of results simpler. The framing of hypotheses and discussion of results are therefore, carried out in terms of each variable of effectiveness which has made the presentation repetitive, at times. Even though the vast insight that I gained at the different stages in exploring this complex field made me wish that the study be redesigned at every stage, but it was impossible! The observations and suggestions given below are based on my experiences during the study.

The study could lay down only the broad parameters along which effectiveness studies in libraries can be conducted. Its findings therefore, need to be supported by further studies conducted by using the same instruments on larger samples.

The study has adopted four different measures for judging the performance of library organisations and it has not been possible to carry out the in-depth study of each organisation using multiple criteria. A criterion like the user's satisfaction needs intensive investigation, in order to make it an effective tool of organisational analysis. The samples of users should be representative of the total population and may require a large number of days of exclusive data collection for this purpose.

The variables chosen for the study highlight the internal system of the organisation. Other variables like adaptability to change, role of unions etc., have not been included in the study. As none of the libraries had initiated computerisation, the impact of the technology also could not be studied.

The study has been designed from a short-time frame of reference, and reports the findings as observed at a particular point of time. However, from an organisational analysis point of view, the longitudinal studies may have more implications. But such studies can not be undertaken without the active interest, involvement and support of the organisation to which the researher is attached. The sample for the study consisted of fifteen libraries in Delhi, drawn initially on the basis of purposive sampling; a much large sample drawn on the all India basis needs to be studied before any generalisation is made about the behaviour of libraries.

Though the framework of the study has been designed to investigate the problems of service organisations, i.e. the libraries, its findings or generalisations cannot be applied to all types of service organisations.

Because of the limited size of the sample in terms of the organisations studied (N—15), it has been possible to report the results only on the basis of correlation analysis between the independent and effectiveness variables. A much larger sample was needed to carry out the regression analysis and to find out the predictors of effectiveness in library organisations.

Though an attempt has been made, in the present study, to simplify and modify the assessment tools so as to make them more sensitive to the Indian situation, the basic guidelines for the study were provided by the studies conducted abroad. The influence of prevalent economic, social and political values on Indian organisations cannot, however, be overlooked (Dayal, 1976). Similar views are expressed by Singh and Kaul (1983) who state that the learning and unlearning processes and the manipulation that occur in the Indian organisations are quite different from the western concepts, and, therefore, different tools are needed for reaching the Indian conditions. The tools used in the study cannot claim the perfect sensitivity of tapping the prevalent culture in Indian organisations.

During the course of investigation, it was observed that the employees, at least, at junior cadres have a tendency to answer the question items from personal rather than organisational perspective. As such an element of subjectivity in the responses could not be ruled out.

The rate of growth index finally consisted of the budget figures of the organisations as the data on the other growth indicators such as increase in membership, circulation records could not be obtained from all the participating organisations. This may, perhaps, account for the insensitivity of this index in being an adequate indicator of real organisational growth. Emphasis is to be laid on objective indications of effectiveness as outlined above to plan more realistic studies.

Important Suggestions

In order to establish the efficacy of organisational assessment instruments used in the study, it is recommended that in-depth studies using suitable criteria should be carried out in library organisations.

During the course of investigation, it was observed that variables like the nature of ownership of the library organisations (whether government-owned or privately registered or autonomous) may have an influence on their functioning. But this aspect could not be investigated for lack of adequate number of samples under each type. Future researches on library effectiveness may investigate into such aspects as the ownership and age of the organisations.

Studies on library effectiveness may be carried out be incorporating variables like adaptability to change (response to external environment) and the role of unions.

Effectiveness studies may also be carried out by using the actual performance figures of the library on various accounts, such as the number of reference queries answered, loans procured from outside, photocopies supplied and number of books issued during a particular period depending upon the availability of data.

During the course of investigation it was also observed that some of the libraries which were high on group performance scale and were rated high by the user's did not provide high job satisfaction and positive climate to its employees. This apparently suggests the prevalence of a personal work ethics among Indian workers which needs further investigation. Future studies may try to incorporate such issues which may throw light on the personality of the Indian worker.

Studies should be conducted, taking data from wide cross-sections of libraries. This will ultimately contribute to the building of theories on library effectiveness.

In the end, it is hoped that my attempt of investigating the complex system of library organisations, even in the face of warning from management experts like Cameron (1980) that there can never be a perfect evaluation of the service organisations, would stimulate young minds to explore this difficult but challenging field. It was my earnest desire to arrive at the predictors of user's satisfaction out of the eight parameters used in the 'user's satisfaction scale'. But due to same initial deficiency in the design of the scale, my efforts did not yield the desired result. I earnestly hope that further studies in this area would be undertaken with suitable modification in research design.

APPENDIX A

Organisation Assessment Survey

Questionnaire-I

This questionnaire relates to organisation Assessment Survey. The purpose of this Survey is to learn more about your organisation structure and various jobs and routines in your library. The information given by you will help in identifying and solving some of the problems faced by your library. The information furnished will be kept strictly confidential. The questionnaire consists of two parts : Section A and Section B.

Section A

Please give information in the space provided against each question. Please circle the relevant information wherever you have to choose between alternative answers, e.g. circle the age group 20-30 if your age falls in this group.

General Information

1. Name of the Library : ——————————
2. Name of the Section in which you are working : ——————————
3. Present Designation : ——————————
4. Designation on joining the library : ——————————

5.	Age (Between)	: 20-30/31-40/41-50/51-60
6.	Sex	: Male/Female
7.	Marital Status	: Married/Unmarried
8.	Educational Qualification	: BA/B.Sc., MA/M.Sc., Ph D.
9.	Professional Qualification	: M.LIB Sc, B. Lib Sc, Certificate, Training in Computer Language.
10.	Work Experience	: Total———years
11.		: In this organisation———years

Section B

In this section you have to circle one of the numbers that appear on a scale below the queston. On top of the scale description is given of what each number represents. Please circle the number which most accurately reflect your answer.

Here is an example :	Rarely	Sometimes	About half the time	Often	Very Often
	1	2	3	4	5

In this example respondent has circled third item on the scale.

1. Do all the employees in your library have clearly defined responsibilities ?

NO ONE	ONLY A FEW	ABOUT HALF	MANY	ALL
1	2	3	4	5

2. Do alll the employees in your library have properly defined reporting system (i.e. he is responsible to one supervisor only) ?

NO ONE	ONLY A FEW	ABOUT HALF	MANY	ALL
1	2	3	4	5

3. Do supervisory staff (Asst. Librarians/Dy, Librarians) in

your organisation have clearly defined authority and responsibility ?

NONE	ONLY A FEW	ABOUT A HALF	MANY	ALL
1	2	3	4	5

4. Is the work distribution among different employees of your library rational ?

NOT AT ALL	VERY LITTLE	SOME WHAT	QUITE A BIT	VERY MUCH
1	2	3	4	5

5. Are the responsibilities of the unit/sub-unit clearly defined ?

NOT AT ALL	VERY LITTLE	SOME WHAT	QUITE A BIT	ALL
1	2	3	4	5

6. Are the related jobs and tasks to be performed kept together while allocating responsibilities among units ?

NONE	ONLY A FEW	ABOUT HALF	MANY	ALL
1	2	3	4	5

7. Necessary cooperation and support comes from other units where work of your units is related to their work.

VERY SELDOM	SOME TIMES	ABOUT HALF THE TIMES	QUITE OFTEN	VERY OFTEN
1	2	3	4	5

8. When a task is to be performed by coordinated efforts of different sections, then the role to be played by each section is clearly defined?

VERY SELDOM	SOME TIMES	ABOUT HALF THE TIMES	QUITE OFTEN	VERY OFTEN
1	2	3	4	5

9. Does the work given to you match your training ?

VERY SELDOM	SOME TIMES	ABOUT HALF THE TIMES	QUITE OFTEN	VERY OFTEN
1	2	3	4	5

10. Does the work given to you match your experience ?

VERY SELDOM	SOME TIMES	ABOUT HALF THE TIMES	QUITE OFTEN	VERY OFTEN
1	2	3	4	5

11. How precisely do the rules and procedures specify the major tasks to be done by you ?

TO NO EXTENT	LITTLE EXTENT	SOME EXTENT	GREAT EXTENT	VERY GREAT EXTENT
1	2	3	4	5

12. How many written rules and procedures exist for doing your major tasks ?

VERY FEW	A SMALL NUMBER	A MODERATE NUMBER	A LARGE NUMBER	A GREAT NUMBER
1	2	3	4	5

13. Once a job is assigned to you, are you left to complete the job your self ?

VERY SELDOM	SOME TIMES	ABOUT HALF THE TIMES	QUITE OFTEN	VERY OFTEN
1	2	3	4	5

14. Is the standard of performance that your management expects from the employee very high ?

NOT AT ALL	SOME WHAT	MODERATELY HIGH	MOSTLY HIGH	VERY HIGH
1	2	3	4	5

15. Do you think people who do well in your organisation are always rewarded ?

NEVER	SOME TIMES	ABOUT HALF THE TIMES	MOST OF THE TIMES	ALWAY
1	2	3	4	5

16. When somebody in the organisation makes mistake the policy of the organisation is to take action depending upon the seriousness of mistake ?

NEVER	SOME TIMES	ABOUT HALF THE TIMES	MOST OF THE TIMES	ALWAYS
1	2	3	4	5

17. If you attain the performance level expected of you, how likely is it that each of the following will happen ?

NO CHANCE	SMALL CHANCE	50% CHANCE	QUITE LIKELY	ALMOST A CERTAINITY
1	2	3	4	5

(a) you will be given promotion

1	2	3	4	5

(b) you will be given recognisation

18. To what extent do you believe that the performance standards upon which your work is evaluated if fair ?

NO STANDARD	VERY UNFAIR	SOME WHAT FAIR	QUITE FAIR	VERY FAIR
1	2	3	4	5

19. How much influence say did each of the following have in deciding upon the criteria for evaluating your performance ?

	NONE	LITTLE	SOME	QUITE A BIT	VERY MUCH
(a) Senior people out side your work unit	1	2	3	4	5
(b) you, as the unit supervisor	1	2	3	4	5

(c) your subordinate individually	1	2	3	4	5
(d) you and subordinate in group meeting	1	2	3	4	5

20. Do you have a system for training of employees in your library ?

VERY RARELY	OCCASIO-NALLY	QUITE OFTEN	VERY OFTEN	REGULARLY
1	2	3	4	5

21. Do you feel training imparted to the employees helps them to perform better ?

TO NO EXTENT	LITTLE EXTENT	SOME EXTENT	GREAT EXTENT	VERY GREAT EXTENT
1	2	3	4	5

22. When an employee joins the library is he aware of the terms and conditions of the service applicable to him ?

NEVER	SOME TIMES	ABOUT HALF THE TIMES	MOST OF THE TIMES	ALWAYS
1	2	3	4	5

23. Do you think the decisions in your library are taken by the participation of all concerned most of the time ?

NEVER	SOME TIMES	ABOUT HALF THE TIMES	MOST OF THE TIMES	ALWAYS
1	2	3	4	5

24. The comments and suggestion of the supervisor complements the problem solving approach and activities of the individual group ?

NEVER	SOME TIMES	ABOUT HALF THE TIMES	MOST OF THE TIMES	ALWAYS
1	2	3	4	5

25. Do you feel that your library makes uses of skills and talents of employees by involving them in decision-making ?

NEVER	SOME TIMES	ABOUT HALF THE TIMES	MOST OF THE TIMES	ALWAYS
1	2	3	4	5

26. Does your librarian always keep employees informed of the policies of the library ?

NEVER	SOME TIMES	ABOUT HALF THE TIMES	MOST OF THE TIMES	ALWAYS
1	2	3	4	5

27. Does your librarian keep all employees informed of the policies of the library ?

VERY FEW	SMALL NUMBER	MODERATE NUMBER	A LARGE NUMBER	A GREAT NUMBER
1	2	3	4	5

28. Does your library have an informal method of communication which helps it to solve many of its day-to-day problems ?

TO NO EXTENT	LITTLE EXTENT	SOME EXTENT	GREAT EXTENT	VERY GREAT EXTENT
1	2	3	4	5

29. Do you feel top management is open to suggestions from the lower level ?

TO NO EXTENT	LITTLE EXTENT	SOME EXTENT	GREAT EXTENT	VERY GREAT EXTENT
1	2	3	4	5

30. Do you think that people at the top are aware of the problems faced by people at the lower levels regarding their work ?

TO NO EXTENT	LITTLE EXTENT	SOME EXTENT	GREAT EXTENT	VERY GREAT EXTENT
1	2	3	4	5

31. To what extent seniors in your library are concerned about the employees ?

TO NO EXTENT	LITTLE EXTENT	SOME EXTENT	GREAT EXTENT	VERY GREAT EXTENT
1	2	3	4	5

32. Do you think the seniors in your library are concerned with work alone ?

TO NO EXTENT	LITTLE EXTENT	SOME EXTENT	GREAT EXTENT	VERY GREAT EXTENT
1	2	3	4	5

33. Do you think the seniors in your library are friendly and approachable ?

TO NO EXTENT	LITTLE EXTENT	SOME EXTENT	GREAT EXTENT	VERY GREAT EXTENT
1	2	3	4	5

34. Do you think in your library when there is a difference of opinion the seniors take active part in resolving the conflict ?

TO NO EXTENT	LITTLE EXTENT	SOME EXTENT	GREAT EXTENT	VERY GREAT EXTENT
1	2	3	4	5

35. To what extent do you feel commited to your job ?

TO NO EXTENT	LITTLE EXTENT	SOME EXTENT	GREAT EXTENT	VERY GREAT EXTENT
1	2	3	4	5

36. Does the senior after assigning the job gives detailed instruction on how to do the job ?

VERY SELDOM	SOME TIMES	ABOUT HALF THE TIMES	QUITE OFTEN	VERY OFTEN
1	2	3	4	5

37. Do you try to meet work standard and see that job is done according to the standard set ?

TO NO EXTENT	LITTLE EXTENT	SOME EXTENT	GREAT EXTENT	VERY GREAT EXTENT
1	2	3	4	5

38. Do you try to take initiative in solving work problems ?

VERY SELDOM	SOME TIMES	ABOUT HALF THE TIMES	QUITE OFTEN	VERY OFTEN
1	2	3	4	5

39. After having performed your job, do you have a sense of achievement ?

VERY SELDOM	SOME TIMES	ABOUT HALF THE TIMES	QUITE OFTEN	VERY OFTEN
1	2	3	4	5

40. How satisfied are you with each of the following ?

	VERY UN-SATIS-FIED	QUITE UN-SATIS-FIED	SOME-WHAT SATIS-FIED	QUITE SATIS-FIED	VERY SATIS-FIED
(a) your job	1	2	3	4	5

(b) your supervisor	1	2	3	4	5
(c) your pay	1	2	3	4	5
(d) the friendliness of co-workers	1	2	3	4	5
(e) the career progress you have made in this library	1	2	3	4	5
(f) your chance for career progress in this library in the future	1	2	3	4	5

41. Each of the following statements indicate something that a person might say about his or her job. Please express your opinion regarding the following :

	DISAGREE STRONGLY	DISAGREE SOME-WHAT	NEUT-RAL	AGREE SOME-WHAT	AGREE STRO-NGLY
(a) my opinion of myself goes up when I do the job well	1	2	3	4	5
(b) I feel a sense of personal accomplishment when I do the job well	1	2	3	4	5

(c)	I regularly think of quitting the job	1	2	3	4	5
(d)	I feel bad and unhappy when I discover that I have poorly performed my job	1	2	3	4	5
(e)	I feel a very high degree of personal responsibility for my job	1	2	3	4	5
(f)	My own feelings are generally not affected much one way or the other by how well I perform the job	1	2	[illegible]	1	5

APPENDIX B

Organisation Assessment Survey

Questionnaire-II

This questionnaire relates to Organisation Assessment Survey. The purpose of this Survey is to learn more about your organisation structure and various jobs and routines in your library. The information given by you will help in identifying and solving some of the problems faced by your library. The information furnished will be kept strictly confidential. The questionnares consists of two parts Section A and SectionB

Section A

Please give information in the space provided against each question. Please circle the relevant information wherever you have to choose between alternative answers, e.g. circle the age group 20-30 if your age falls in this group.

General Information

1. Name of the Library : ——————————————
2. Name of the Section in which you are working : ——————————————
3. Present Designation : ——————————————
4. Designation on joining the library : ——————————————
5. Age (Between) : 20-30/31-40/41-50/51-60

6. **Sex** : **Male/Female**
7. Marital Status : Married/Unmarried
8. Educational Qualification : Matric/Intermediate/BA/B.Sc., MA/M.Sc./Ph.D.
9. Professional Qualification : M.LIB Sc./B. Lib Sc/Certificate, Training in Computer Language.
10. Work Experience : ————————Years

Section B

In this section you have to circle one of the numbers that appear on a scale below the question. On top of the scale description is given of what each number represents. Please circle the number which most accurately reflect your answer.

Here is an Example :

Rarely	Sometimes	About Half The Time	Often	Very Often
1	2	3	4	5

In this example respondent has circled third item on the Scale.

1. Do all the employees in your library have clearly defined *responsibilities* ?

NONE	ONLY A FEW	ABOUT HALF	MANY	ALL
1	2	3	4	5

2. Do all the employees in your library have properly defined *reporting system* (i.e. he is responsible to one supervisor only) ?

NONE	ONLY A FEW	ABOUT HALF	MANY	ALL
1	2	3	4	5

3. Is there fair *distribution of work* among different employees of your library

NOT AT ALL	VERY LITTLE	SOME WHAT	QUITE A BIT	VERY MUCH
1	2	3	4	5

4. Are the responsibilities of the *units/sub—units* clearly defined ?

NOT AT ALL	VERY LITTLE	SOME WHAT	QUITE A BIT	ALL
1	2	3	4	5

5. Are the *related jobs and task* kept together while allocating responsibilities among units ?

NONE	ONLY A FEW	ABOUT HALF	MANY	ALL
1	2	3	4	5

6. When a task is to be performed by *coordinated efforts* of different sections is the *role to be played by each section clearly defined then* ?

VERY SELDOM	SOME TIMES	ABOUT HALF THE TIMES	QUITE OFTEN	VERY OFTEN
1	2	3	4	5

7. Does the work given to you match your training ?

VERY SELDOM	SOME TIMES	ABOUT HALF THE TIMES	QUITE OFTEN	VERY OFTEN
1	2	3	4	5

8. Does the work given to you match your experience ?

VERY SELDOM	SOME TIMES	ABOUT HALF THE TIMES	QUITE OFTEN	VERY OFTEN
1	2	3	4	5

9. How precisely do the *rules and procedures specify the major tasks* to be done by you ?

TO NO EXTENT	LITTLE EXTENT	SOME EXTENT	GREAT EXTENT	VERY GREAT EXTENT
1	2	3	4	5

10. How many *written rules and procedures* exist for doing your major tasks ?

VERY FEW	A SMALL NUMBER	A MODERATE NUMBER	A LARGE NUMBER	A GREAT NUMBER
1	2	3	4	5

11. Do you think people who do well in your organisation are always rewarded ?

NEVER	SOME TIMES	ABOUT HALF THE TIME	MOST OF THE TIMES	ALWAYS
1	2	3	4	5

12. When somebody in the organisation makes mistake is the policy of the organisation is to take action depending upon the seriousness of mistake ?

NEVER	SOME TIMES	ABOUT HALF THE TIME	MOST OF THE TIMES	ALWAYS
1	2	3	4	5

13. To what extent do you believe that the performance standards upon which your work is evaluated is fair ?

NO STAN-DARD AT ALL	VERY UNFAIR	SOME WHAT FAIR	QUITE FAIR	VERY FAIR
1	2	3	4	5

14. If you attain the performance level expected of you, are you given promotion ?

NO CHANCE	SMALL CHANCE	50% CHANCE	QUITE LIKELY	ALMOST A CERTAINITY
1	2	3	4	5

15. Does your library has a policy on training of the employees ?

VERY RARELY	OCCASIO-NALLY	QUITE OFTEN	VERY OFTEN	REGULA-RLY
1	2	3	4	5

16. Do you feel training imparted to the employees helps them to perform better ?

TO NO EXTENT	LITTLE EXTENT	SOME EXTENT	GREAT EXTENT	VERY GREAT EXTENT
1	2	3	4	5

17. Do you think the decisions in your library are taken by the participation of all concerned most of the time ?

NEVER	SOME TIME	ABOUT HALF THE TIME	MOST OF THE TIMES	ALWAYS
1	2	3	4	5

18. Do you feel that your library makes use of skills and talents of employees by involving them in decision-making ?

NEVER	SOME TIMES	ABOUT HALF THE TIME	MOST OF THE TIMES	ALWAYS
1	2	3	4	5

19. Do you feel top management is open to suggestions from the lower level ?

TO NO EXTENT	LITTLE EXTENT	SOME EXTENT	GREAT EXTENT	VERY GREAT EXTENT
1	2	3	4	5

20. Does the seniors in your library keep the concerned employees informed of the policies of the library ?

VERY SELDOM	SOME TIMES	ABOUT HALF THE TIME	QUITE OFTEN	VERY OFTEN
1	2	3	4	5

21. Do you think seniors in your library are aware of the problems faced by the people at lower levels regarding their work ?

TO NO EXTENT	LITTLE EXTENT	SOME EXTENT	GREAT EXTENT	VERY GREAT EXTENT
1	2	3	4	5

22. Does there exist in your library an informal method of communication which helps it to solve many of its day-to-day problems ?

TO NO EXTENT	LITTLE EXTENT	SOME EXTENT	GREAT EXTENT	VERY GREAT EXTENT
1	2	3	4	5

23. To what an extent seniors in your library are concerned about the employees ?

TO NO EXTENT	LITTLE EXTENT	SOME EXTENT	GREAT EXTENT	VERY GREAT EXTENT
1	2	3	4	5

24. Do you think seniors in your library are friendly and approachable ?

TO NO EXTENT	LITTLE EXTENT	SOME EXTENT	GREAT EXTENT	VERY GREAT EXTENT
1	2	3	4	5

25. Do you think seniors in your library are concerned with work alone ?

VERY GREAT EXTENT	GREAT EXTENT	SOME EXTENT	LITTLE EXTENT	TO NO EXTENT
1	2	3	4	5

26. Does the senior after assigning the job gives detailed instruction on how to do the job ?

VERY SELDOM	SOME TIMES	ABOUT HALF THE TIME	QUITE OFTEN	VERY OFTEN
1	2	3	4	5

27. Do you think in your library seniors take active part in resolving the conflict when there is difference of opinion among the employees ?

VERY SELDOM	SOME TIMES	ABOUT HALF THE TIME	QUITE OFTEN	VERY OFTEN
1	2	3	4	5

28. Do you think the suggestion of the supervisor complements the problem solving approach of the individuals/group ?

VERY SELDOM	SOME TIMES	ABOUT HALF THE TIME	QUITE OFTEN	VERY OFTEN
1	2	3	4	5

29. To what an extent do you find the working condition in your library as satisfactory ?

TO NO EXTENT	LITTLE EXTENT	SOME EXTENT	GREAT EXTENT	VERY GREAT EXTENT
1	2	3	4	5

30. Do you receive cooperation and support from your co-workers when needed ?

VERY SELDOM	SOME TIMES	ABOUT HALF THE TIME	QUITE OFTEN	VERY OFTEN
1	2	3	4	5

31. Do you try to meet work standard and see that the job is done according to the standard set ?

TO NO EXTENT	LITTLE EXTENT	SOME EXTENT	GREAT EXTENT	VERY GREAT EXTENT
1	2	3	4	5

32. Do you try to take initiative in solving work problems ?

VERY SELDOM	SOME TIMES	ABOUT HALF THE TIME	QUITE OFTEN	VERY OFTEN
1	2	3	4	5

33. Once a job is assigned to you, are you left to complete the job by yourself ?

VERY SELDOM	SOME TIMES	ABOUT HALF THE TIME	QUITE OFTEN	VERY OFTEN
1	2	3	4	5

34. Do you feel bad and unhappy when you discover that you have poorly performed your job ?

TO NO EXTENT	LITTLE EXTENT	SOME EXTENT	GREAT EXTENT	VERY GREAT EXTENT
1	2	3	4	5

35. Do you have a sense of belonging to the library in which you are working ?

TO NO EXTENT	LITTLE EXTENT	SOME EXTENT	GREAT EXTENT	VERY GREAT EXTENT
1	2	3	4	5

36. Given an opportunity would you like to leave this organisation and join some other organisation?

NEVER	SOME TIMES	ABOUT HALF THE TIME	MOST OF THE TIMES	ALWAYS
1	2	3	4	5

Section B

Name of the Library

1. Collection

1.1. Do you find the collections of the library in your field of interest adequate ?

INADE-QUATE	PARTI-ALLY INADE-QUATE	MODERA-TELY ADEQUATE	PAR-TIALLY ADEQUATE	ADEQUATE
1	2	3	4	5

1.2. How up-to-date do you find the library collection ?

NOT AT ALL UPTO DATE	LITTLE UPTO DATE	MODERA-TELY UPTO DATE	QUITE UPTO DATE	VERY UPTO DATE
1	2	3	4	5

2. Efficiency of Procurement and Processing

2.1. Does the library acquire the material requested in reasonable period of time ?

VERY UNREA-SONABLE	UNREA-SONABLE	MODERA-TELY REASO-NABLE	PARTI-ALLY REASO-NABLE	REASO-NABLE
5	2	3	4	5

2.2. Does the library process (i.e. place on shelves for use of readers) the material acquired in reasonable period of time ?

VERY UNREASONABLE	UNREASONABLE	MODERATELY REASONABLE	PARTIALLY REASONABLE	REASONABLE
1	2	5	4	5

3. **Library Records**

3.1. Are you satisfied with the various records of the library that help you in getting the materials/information you want ?

VERY UNSATISFIED	QUITE UNSATISFIED	SOMEWHAT SATISFIED	QUITE SATISFIED	VERY SATISFIED
1	2	3	4	5

3.2. How useful do you find the library catalogue ?

NOT AT ALL USEFUL	LITTLE USEFUL	MODERATELY USEFUL	QUITE USEFUL	VERY USEFUL
1	2	3	4	5

4. **Sources of Information**

4.1. Does the library has adequate collection of the information sources such as Abstracts Indexes and Bibliographies in your area of interest ?

INADEQUATE	PARTIALLY INADEQUATE	MODERATELY ADEQUATE	PARTIALLY ADEQUATE	ADEQUATE
1	2	3	4	5

4.2. Does the library has adequate number of sources such as Union Catalogues that guide you to the collection of other libraries ?

INADE-QUATE	PARTI-ALLY INADE-QUATE	MODERA-TELY ADEQUATE	PARTI-ALY ADE-QUATE	ADE-QUATE
1	2	3	4	5

5. **Arrangement on Shelves**

5.2. Are you satisfied with the arrangement of materials on the shelves ?

VERY UN-SATISFIED	QUITE UN-SATISFIED	SOME WHAT SATIS-FIED	QUITE SATISFIED	VERY SATIS-FIED
1	2	3	4	5

5.2. How often are you able to locate the material on the shelves ?

VERY SELDOM	SOME TIMES	ABOUT HALF THE TIME	QUITE OFTEN	VERY OFTEN
1	2	3	4	5

6. **Services Provided by the Library**

6.1. How much satisfied do you feel with the reference services (on spot assistance) provided by the library ?

VERY UN-SATISFIED	QUITE UN-SATISFIED	SOME-WHAT SATIS-FIED	QUITE SATISFIED	VERY SATIS-FIED
1	2	3	4	5

6.2. How much satisfied do you feel with the special services such as photocopying, inter-library loan etc. provided by the library ?

VERY UN-SATISFIED	QUITE UN-SATISFIED	SOME WHAT SATIS-FIED	QUITE SATISFIED	VERY SATIS-FIED
1	2	3	4	5

7. **Assistance from the Library Staff**

7.1. Do you seek the assistance from library staff from time when you face difficulties in the library ?

VERY SELDOM	SOME TIMES	ABOUT HALF THE TIME	QUITE OFTEN	VERY OFTEN
1	2	3	4	5

7.2. Do you find the library staff helpful ?

NOT AT ALL HELPFUL	LITTLE HELPFUL	MODERA-TELY HELPFUL	QUITE HELPFUL	VERY HELPFUL
1	2	3	4	5

8. **Satisfaction with the Library Timings**

8.1. How much satisfied do you feel with the present opening and closing hours of the library ?

VERY UN-SATISFIED	QUITE UN-SATISFIED	SOME-WHAT SATIS-FIED	QUITE SATIS-FIED	VERY SATIS-FIED
1	2	3	4	5

8.2. How much satisfied do you feel with present working hours on Sundays and Holidays. ?

VERY UN-SATISFIED	QUITE UN-SATISFIED	SOME-WHAT SATIS-FIED	QUITE SATIS-FIED	VERY SATIS-FIED
1	2	3	4	5

APPENDIX C

Employee's Job Satisfaction Scale

(Developed and evaluated by Taylor and Bowers (1972) and Modified by Van De Ven and Ferry (1980)

How satisfied do you feel with each of the following at your working place ?

	VERY UN-SATIS-FIED	QUITE UN-SATIS-FIED	SOME-WHAT SATIS-FIED	QUITE SATIS-FIED	VERY SATIS-FIED
1. Your Job	1	2	3	4	5
2. Your supervisor	1	2	3	4	5
3. Your pay	1	2	3	4	5
4. The friendliness of co-workers	1	2	3	4	5
5. The career progress you have made in this library	1	2	3	4	5
6. Yours chances for career progress in this library in the furture	1	2	3	4	5

APPENDIX D

Group Performance Scale

(To be filled by Division/Section Heads)

How will you rate the following attributes while describing the performance of the group working under you ?

	V. Low	Low	Average	High	V. High
1. Work performance	1	2	3	4	5
2. Job knowledge of the team members	1	2	3	4	5
3. Initiative taken in discharging responsibilities	1	2	3	4	5
4. Cooperation among the team members	1	2	3	4	5
5. Reliability of the group on the whole	1	2	3	4	5

6. Leadership traits among the team members	1	2	3	4	5

Note : 1. **Work Performance**

Results achieved considering the amount of effort application and time taken.

2. **Job Knowledge**

Knowledge of methods, procedures in relation to the job, any other knowledge of the procedures and policies of the organisation as required by his position.

3. **Initiative**

Resourcefulness, imagination and ability to develop new ideas, improved approaches to work problems.

4. **Cooperation**

Willingness to extend cooperation to others and ability to receive cooperation from others.

5. **Reliability**

Accomplishes agreed targets without goading or giving room to anxiety.

6. **Leadership**

Success in stimulating and motivating subordinates, delegating responsibility efficiently and create harmonious work group.

APPENDIX E

Organisational Record Profile

1. **History**

   (i) Name of the parent body ______________

   (ii) Name of the Library ______________

   (iii) Year of establishment ______________

2. **Collection**

   (i) Books ______________

   (ii) Journals ______________

   (iii) Special collection ______________

   (iv) Other types ______________

   (v) Total ______________

3. **Budget**

   (i) Books ______________

   (ii) Journals ______________

   (iii) Other Heads ______________

   (iv) Total ______________

4. **Staffiing Pattern**

	No.	**Pay Scale**
(i) Librarian	______	________
(ii) Dy. Librarian	______	________
(iii) Asst. Librarian	______	________
(iv) Professional Asst.	______	________
(v) Semi professional Asst.	______	________

(vi) Attendants ______ ________
(vii) Clerical ______ ________
(viii) Others ______ ________
(ix) Total ______ ________

5. Work Organisation

	Name of Section	*Functions*	*Staff Allocated*				
			Dy. Librarian	*Asst. Lib.*	*Lib. Asst.*	*Attendants*	*Others*
(i)	____	____	____	____	____	____	____
(ii)	____	____	____	____	____	____	____
(iii)	____	____	____	____	____	____	____
(iv)	____	____	____	____	____	____	____
(v)	____	____	____	____	____	____	____

6. Membership

Students ______________
Staff ______________
Others ______________
Total ______________

Bibliography

Agrawal, K.G. 1975 : Organisational Variables Influencing Hospital Performance. *Indian Journal of Industrial Relations*, 11 : 29-39.

Ansari, M.A. and Rub, M. 1982: Executive Success as a Function of Leadership Style-Organisational Climate Fit. *Managerial Psychology*, 3 : 56-58.

Argyris, Chris, 1964 : Integrating the Individual and Organisation, New York, Wiley.

Bajaj, P. 1981 : Alienation as Related to Perception of Organisational Climate. *Indian Journal of Industrial Relations*, 17 : 563-572.

Bakhru, H.J. 1963 : Effective Employer Communication. *Indian Management*, 2 : 29-31.

Bardford, L. P. 1978 : Group Formation and Development in P. Bardford (Ed) : *Group Development*. La Jolla, University Associates.

Barker, R.G. and Gump, P.V. (Ed.), 1964 : *Big Schools, Small Schools : High School Size and Student Behaviour*. Palo Alto, California, Stanford University Press.

Beckhard, R. 1969 : *Organisation Development : Strategies and Models*. Reading Mass., Addision-Wesley.

Bennis, W.G., 1962 : Towards a 'Truly' Scientific Management: The Concept of Organisational Health. *General Systems Year Book*, p. 269-282

Bernard, C.I., 1938: *Functions of Executive.* Cambridge, Harvard University Press.

Bhattacharjee, K.K., 1979 : Public Library as Social Institution : How it can Function up in K.K. Bhattacharjee (Ed) : *Modern Trends in Librarianship in India.* Calcutta, World Press.

Bhooshan Lal, 1984: *Factors Related to Employee Performance.* Ph.D. Thesis, Indian Institute of Technology, Delhi.

Blagden, John, 1980: *Do We Really Need Libraries* ? New York, Clive Bingley.

Blake, Robert R. and Mouton, Jane, S., 1964 : *The Managerial Grid.* Houston, Tex., Gulf Publishing.

Blake, Robert R. and Mounton, Jane, S., 1969 : *Building a Dynamic Corporation Through Grid Organisation Development.* Reading, Mass., Addision Wesley.

Blau, Peter M. and Scott W. Richard, 1962 : *Formal Organisations : A Comparative Approach*, San Francisco, Chandler.

Blau, Peter M. and Schoenherr, Richard W. 1971 : *The Structure of the Organisations*, New York, Basic Books.

Blau, Peter M. et al., 1966 : The Structure of Small Bureaucracies. *American Sociological Review*, 31 : 179-91.

Blough, Rogar, M., 1964 : Libraries and Space Age In Donald H. Hunt (Ed) : *Libraries and Reading : Essays.* Philadelphia, Drexel Press.

Boswell, J., 1973 : *The Rise and Decline of Small Firms.* London, Allen and Unwin.

Brown, J.M. et al. 1966 : *Applied Psychology*, New Delhi, Amering.

Burges, Lyne A. 1970 : Motivation : Key to Non-use of Academic Library. In *Proceedings of New York Library Association Conference* p., 25-29.

Burns, T. and Stalker, G.M., 1961 : *The Management of Innovation.* London, Tavistock.

Burr, R.L., 1957 : Library Goals and Behaviour. *Collage and Research Libraries*, 36 : 27-32,

Butler, Pierce, 1933 : *Introduction to Library Science.* Chicago, University Press.

Cameron, Kim, 1978 : Measuring Organisational Effectiveness in Institution of Higher Learning. *Administrative Science Quarterly*, 24 : 604-34.

Cameron, Kim, 1980 : Critical Questions in Assessing Organisational Effectiveness. Boulder, Amacon, a division of American Management Association.

Cameron, K.M., 1981 : Domains of Organisational Effectiveness in Colleges and Universities. *Academy of Management Journal*, 24 : 25-28.

Cameron, Kim S., 1983 : *Investigating the Causal Association between Unionism and Organisational Effectiveness Boulder* National Center for Higher Management Systems.

Campbell, J.P. and Beaty, E.E.,1971 : Organisational Climate : Its Measurement and Relationship to work Group Performance : Paper presented at the Annual Meeting of the Amercan Psychological Association, Washington.

Campbell, John, 1977 : On the Nature of Organisational Effectiveness In Paul S. Goodman et al. (Ed.) : *New Perspective in Organisation Effectiveness.* San Francisco, Jossey Boss, p. 13-16.

Champney, H., 1941 : The Measurement of Parent Behaviour. *Child Development*, 12 : 131-66.

Chatterjee, A. and James, E.V., 1965 : An Investigation into the Problem of Effective Supervision. *Journal of Indian Academy af Applied Psychology*, 2 : 8 12.

Child, J., 1973 : Strategies of Control and Organisational Behaviour. *Administrative Science Quarterly*, 18 : 1-17.

Child, J., 1974 : Managerial and Organisational Factors Associated with Company Performance Pt. I. *Journal of Management Studies*, 11 : 175-89.

Child, J., 1975 : Managerial and Organisational Factors Associated with Company Performance Pt. II. *Journal of Management Studies*, 12: 12-27.

Choudhury, Kamla, 1965 : Worker Participation in Production Problems. *Proceedings of the First Management Conference*, Ahmedabad, ATIRA : 43-46.

Chung, Kae and Meggison, H. 1981 : *Organisational Beha-*

viour : Developing Managerial Skills, New York, Harper and Row.

Cohen, Allen R. et al., 1980 : *Effective Behaviour in Organisations*, Revised edition. Homewood, Illiones, Richard D. Irwin.

Coutler, P.B., 1979 : Organisational Effectiveness in Public Sector. *Administrative Science Quarterly*, 24 : 65-81.

Cumming, S.L.L., 1983 : Organisational Effectiveness and Organisational Behaviour In Kim S. Cameron and Devid Whetten (Ed.) *Organisctional Effectiveness : A Comparison Models*. New York, Academic Press.

Dayal, Ishwar, 1976 : *Change in Work Organisation : Experiences of Renewal in Social System*, Delhi, Concept.

Dearborn, D.C. and Simon, H.A., 1958 : Selective Perception. *Sociometry*, 21 : 140-44.

Drucker, P.E., 1974 : *New Templates in Today's Organisation in Developing Effective Organisations* : Harvard Business Review Report Series, Jan.-Feb., p. 115-123.

Drucker, Peter, 1973 : Managing the Public Service Institutions. *Public Interest*, 33 : 53-60.

Etzioni, Amitai, 1960 : Two Approaches to Organisational Analysis. *Administrative Science Quarterly*, 10 : 1975.

Etzioni, Amitai, 1964 : *Modern Organisations*. New Delhi, Prentice Hall.

Evans, Edward, 1983 : *Management Techniques for Libraries*. New York, Academic Press.

Filley, A.C. and House, R.J. 1969 : *Managerial Process and Organisational Behaviour*. Glenview Illionos, Scott Foresman and Company.

Franklin, Jerome L. 1975 : Relation among four Social Psychological Aspects of Organisations. *Administrative Science Quarterly*, 20 : 422-33.

Frederickson, N., 1966 : *Some Effects of Organisational Climate on Administrative Performance* (ETSRM-66-21), Princetion, N.J., Educational Testing Service.

Friedlander, F. and Marguiles, N. 1969 : Multiple Impact of Organisational Climate and Individual Value System upon Job Satisfaction. *Personnel Psychology*, 22 : 171-83.

Friedlander, F. and Pickle, H., 1968 : Components of Effectiveness in Small Organisations: *Administrative Science Quarterly*, 13 : 289-304.

Georgopoulos, B.S. and Tennenbaum, A.S., 1975 : The study of Organisational Effectiveness. *American Sociological Review*, 22 : 534-40.

Gibson, J.L., Ivancevich, J.M. and Donnelly, J..H., 1973 : *Organisations Structure, Process and Behaviour*. Dallas, Business Publication.

Gilsson, C. and Martin, P.V., 1980 : Productivity and Efficiency in Human Service Organisations as Related to Structure, Size and Age. *Academy of Management Journal*, 23 : 91-37.

Graen, G., 1976 : Role Making Processes within Complex Organisations. In M.D. Dunnette (Ed). *Handbook of Industrial and Organisational Psychology*. Chicago, Rand Mc Nally.

Grewal, T.S., 1963 : Autonomy vs Democracy in Management, *Indian Mangement* 2 : 33-35.

Goldsmith, Walter and Clutterbuck, David, 1984 : *The Winning Streak*. London, Weidenfeld and Nicolson.

Guilford, J. P., 1954 : *Psychometric Methods*, 2nd ed. New York McGraw-Hill.

Guilford, J.P. and Fruchter, B., 1978 : Fundamental Statistics in Psychology and Education, 6th Edition. New Delhi, McGraw-Hill Kogakusha.

Gupta, B.M. et al. (Ed.) 1984 : *Handbook of Libraries Archieves and Information Centres in India*. V.I. New Delhi, Information Industry.

Hackman, J. Richard, 1976 : The Design of Self-Managing Work Group, Technical Report No. 11, New Haven, Yale University, School of Organisation and Management.

Hackman, J. Richard and Lawler Edward E., 1971 : Employee Reaction to Job Characteristics. *Journal of Applied Psychology, Monograph* 55 : 259-86.

Hackman, J. Richard and Oldham, Greg R., 1975 : Development of Job Diagonistic Survey. *Journal of Applied Psychology*, 60 : 159-70.

Hall, Richard H., 1972 : *Organisations, Structure, and Process*, Englewood Cliff, New Jersey, Prentice Hall.

Hall, R.H. et al., 1967 : Examination of the Blau-Scott and

Etzionai Typologies, *Administrative Science Quarterly*, 12 : 118-139.

Hall, Richard H. et al., 1977 : Patterns of Inter-organisational Relationships, *Administrative Science Quarterly*, 22 : 457-77.

Hannabuss, Stuart, 1983 : Measuring the Value and Marketing the Service: An Approach to Library Benefit. Procedings, 35, 418-425.

Hawgood, J. and Morely, R., 1969 : Project for Evaluating the Benefits from University Libraries, Durham University OSTI Report 5056.

Herzberg, F., Hausner, B. and Snyderman, B., 1959: *The Motivation to Work.* New York, Wiley.

Hickson, et al., 1971 : Strategic Contingencies Theory of Intra-organisational Power. *Administrative Science Quarterly*, 16: 216-219.

House, R.J., 1963: *A Predictive Theory of Management Development.* Ann Arbor, Univ. of Michigan, Bureau of Industrial Relations.

Jhuney, S.C., 1976 : Orientation for Workers' Participation in Management, *Indian Journal of Industrial Relations*, 12 : 213.

Kanungo, R.N., 1979 : Concept of Alienation and Involvement Revisited. *Psychological Bulletion*, 86 : 119-138.

Kast, Fremont, E. and Rosenzweic, James E., 1981: *Organisation and Managemeni : A System Contingency Approach*, 3rd edition. New Delhi, McGraw-Hill International.

Katz, Daniel and Kahn, Robert L., 1966 : *The Social Psychology of Organisations*, New Delhi, Wiley Eastern.

Kelly, Joe, 1970: *Make Confiict Work for You In Leadership Pt. I* : Harvard Business Review Reprint Series Reprinted from H.B.R. July-Aug., p. 47-57.

Kent, Allen and Galvin, Thomas J. Ed., 1982 : *Information Technology : Critical Choices for Library Decision Makers.* New York, Marcel Dekkar.

Kent et al. (Ed.), 1980: *Encyclopedia of Library and Information Science V 28.* New York, Marcel Dekkar.

Khandwalla, P.N., 1973 : Viable and Effective Organisational Designs of Firms. *Academy of Management Journal*, 16 : 481-496.

King, D.W. and Bryant, Edward, 1971. *The Evaluation of*

Information Service and Products. Information Resources Press.

King, D.W. and Palmer, V.E., 1973 : *Users Behaviour in Changing Patterns in Information Retrieval.* American Society for Information Science.

Knowles, M.C., 1975 : Inter-dependence among Organisational Variables. *Human Relations*, 28 : 431-449.

Lanceaster, F. W., 1977 : *The Measurement and Evaluation of Library Services.* Information Resources Press.

Lal, B. 1982 : Organisational Climate in Academic Libraries in India : A Pilot Survey. *ILA Bulletin*, 18 : 4-13.

Lawler, E.E. et al., 1974 : Organisational Climate : Relationship to Organisational Structure, Process and Performance, *Organisational Behaviour and Human Performance*, 11 : 139-55.

Likert, Rensis, 1961 : *New Patterns of Management*, New York, McGraw-Hill.

Litwin, G. and Stringer, R., 1968 : *Motivation and Organisational Climate.* Cambridge, Mass, Harvard University Press.

Livingston, J. Sterling, 1969 : *Pygmanlian, in Management in Leadership Pt. II* : Harvard Business Review Series Reprinted from H.B.R. July-August, 102-110.

Locke, E.A., 1976 : The Nature and Causes of Job Satisfaction In Marvin D. Dunnette (Ed) : *Handbook of Industrial and Organisational Psychology.* Chicago, Illinois, Rand-McNally.

Luthans, Freed, 1972 : *Organisational Behaviour, International Edition.* New Delhi, McGraw-Hill.

Malviya, Pratibha, 1977 : Perception of Participation in Departmental Decision-making. *Indian Journal of Industrial Relations* : 12 : P. 422.

March, James, G, and Simon, Herbet A., 1958 : *Organisations.* New York, Wiley.

Marrow, A. Bowers, D. and Seashore, S., 1967 : *Management by Participation*, New York, Hauper & Row.

Maslow, Abrahan H., 1954 : *Motivation and Personality.* New York, Harper & Raw.

McColvin, L.R., 1942 : Report on Public Library System of Great Britain. London, Library Association.

McMurry, Rober, N., 1965 : Clear Communications for Chief Executive In *Effective Communications : Harvard Business Review* Reprint Series Reprinted from H.B.R. March-April p. 70-84.

Melcher, Arlyn J., 1976 : *Structure and Process of Organisations.* Englewood Cliffs, New Jersey, Printice-Hall.

Mishra, R., 1982 : Autonomy and Effectiveness : Cases of Government Corporations. *National Labour Institute Bulletin*, 8 : 206-209.

Mott, Paul E., 1972 : *The Characteristics of Effective Organisation.* New York, Harper and Row.

Nand Satya, 1968 : Organisation Structure : A Case Study, *Indian Management*, 7 : 38-41.

Negandhi, A.R. and Reimann, B.C., 1973 : Task Environment, Decentralization and Organisational Effectiveness. *Human Relations*, 26 : 203-14.

Nemiroff, P.M. and Ford, D.L., 1976 : Task Effectiveness and Human Fulfilment in Organisations. *Academy of Management Review*, 1 : 69-82.

Newman, John, E., 1975 : Understanding the Organisation Structure Job Attitude Relationship through Perception of Work Environment. *Organisation Behaviour and Human Performance*, 14 : 371-97.

Oldman, Christine, M., 1978: *The Value of Academic Libraries: A Methodological Investigation*, Ph. D. Thesis, Cranefield Institute of Technology.

Orr, R.H., 1979 : Measuring the Goodness of Library Service : General Framework for Considering Quantitative Measures. *Journal of Documentation*, 29 : 315-330.

Osburn, R.N. and Hunt, J.G., 1974 : Environment and Organisational Effectiveness. *Administrative Science Quarterly*, 19 : 231-46.

Padaki, R., 1984 : Organisational Climate : The Relationship with Employee Satisfaction and Organisational Effection In *Indian Association of Applied Psychology Conference*, New Delhi.

Pareek, U. and Lynton, R.P., 1965 : Senstivity for Personnel and Organisational Development. *Indian Management*, 4 : 40-45.

Patel, V.G. and Srivastava, Anil, 1978 : Small Enterprize Performance—Relevance of Managerial Competence, *ASCI Journal of Management*, 7: 136-150.

Pearce, John and David, Fred, R., 1983 : Social Network Approach to Organisational Design-Performance. *Academy of Management Review*, 8 : 436-444.

Pennigs, J.M., 1975 : The Relevance of Structural Contingency Model for Organisational Effectiveness. *Administrative Science Quarterly*, 20 : 393-410.

Perrow, C.A., 1967 : A Framework for Comparative Analysis of Organisations. *American Sociological Review*, 32 : 194-208.

Peters, Thomas J. and Waterman, Robert, H., 1982 : *In Search of Excellence*, New York, Harper and Row.

Pierce, Jon, L., 1978 : Employee Affective Responses to Work Unit Structure and Job Design. Unpublished Paper. University of Minnesota, School of Business and Administration cited in Van de Ven & Ferry (1980).

Price, J.L., 1968 : *Organisational Effectiveness* : *An Inventory of Propositions* : Homewood, Illinois, Richard D. Irwin Incorporation.

Porter, L.W., 1958 : Differential Self Perceptions of Management Personnel and Line Workers. *Journal of Applied Psychology*, 42 : 105-09.

Porter, L.W. and Lawler, E.E., 1968 : *Managerial Attitude and Behaviour*, Homewood Illinois, Richard D. Irwin, Incorporation.

Porter, L.W. and Steers, R.M., 1973 : Organisational, work and Personal Factors in Employee Turnover and Absenteeism. *Psychological Bulletin*, 80 : 151-76.

Porter, L.W. et al., 1975 : *Behaviour In Organisations*. International Student edition. Tokyo, McGraw Hill Kogakusha.

Ranganathan, S.R., 1931 : *Five Laws of Library Science*, revised edition, published in 1963. Bombay, Asia Publishing.

Raven, B.H. and Rietsema, J., 1957 : Effects of Varied Clarity of Group Path upon the Individual and his Relationship to his Group. *Human Relations*, 10 : 29-45.

Ravens, R.W., 1959 : Human Relation Management and Size. In Hugh-Jones (Ed.) : *Human Relation and Modern Management*. Chicago, Qvodrangle Books.

Robert, Sydney, 1959 : *Roberts Report*, London, H.M.S.Q.

Robock, S.H., 1962 : Management in Underdeveloped Countries. *Advanced Management*, 1 : 31-34.

Roos, N.P. et al., 1974 : Hospital Performance : Analysing Power and Goals. *Journal of Health and Social Behaviour*, 15 : 78-92.

Saha, K., 1989 : Organisational development as a stretagy for library development. *ILA Bulletin*, 23 : 1-7.

Saha, K. 1979 : Controversy of Longer Hours : A Survey at I.I.T. Delhi, *Library Herald*, 18 : 61-68.

Sahoo, K.C., 1978 : Users Survey Concerning Teachers and Research Scholars using Indian Institute of Technology (Delhi) Library. M. Lib. Project, Deptt. of Lib. Sc., Delhi University.

Sayeed, O.B. and Vishwanathan, R. 1983 : Job Characteristics in Relation to Organisational Effectiveness in two Organisations. *Indian Journal of Industrial Relations*, 19 : 57-68.

Schein, Edgar H., 1976: *Organisational Psychology*. 2nd edition, N.D. Prentice-Hall.

Schneider, Benjamin, 1983 : An Interactionist Perspective on Organisational Effectiveness In Kim S. Cameron and D.A. Whetten (Eds.) : *A Comparison Multiple Models*. Academic Press.

Sengupta, Anil, K., 1969 : Some Factors of Malfunctioning of an Industrial Organisation. *Sociological Bulletin*, 17 : 122-38.

Sequeria, C.E., 1964 : Organisational Climate in Indian Industry. *Indian Management*, 3 : 38-40.

Sharma, Chanderkant, 1977 : *Management and Organisational Pattern of University Libraries in M.P.*, India, Ph. D. Thesis, Ravishankaran University.

Sharan, N.K. 1968 : The Climate of an Organisation. *Indian Management*, 7 : 51-56.

Simsova, Sylva, 1982 : *A Primer of Comparative Librarianship*. London, Clive Bingley.

Shintre, J.P., 1967 : A Study of Communication between Management and Employees. *Indian Journal of Social Work* 28 : 329-34.

Singh, N.K. and Pual, Omita, 1985 : *Corporate Soul*. Delhi, Vikas Publishing.

Singh, N.K. and Kaul, Rajani, 1983 : *Key Issues in Organisational Research*, Abhigyan, Spring : 1-16.

Shull, F.A. Delbecq, A.L. and Cummings, I.L., 1970 : *Organisation Decision Making*. New York, McGraw-Hill.

Steers, R.M., 1975 : Task-Goal Attributes in Achievement and Supervisory Performance. *Organisational Behaviour and Human Performance*. 13 : 392-403.

Steers, R.M., 1976 : Factors Affecting Job Attitudes in Goal-setting Environment. *Academy of Management Journal*, 19 : 6-16.

Steers, R.M., 1977 : *Organisational Effectiveness : A Behavioural View*. Santa Monica, California, Good Year Publishing.

Steers, R.M. and Porter, L.W., 1974 : The Role of Task-goal Attributes in Employee Performance. *Psychological Bulletin* 81 : 434-52.

Sunderarajan, V., 1984 : *Organisational Effeciiveness : A study on a public and private organisation*, Ph. D. thesis, I.I.T. Delhi.

Sudame, G.R., 1972 : *Study of the Effect of Library Use on Academic Achievement of Postgraduate Students*, in MS University of Baroda. Ph. D. Thesis, M.S.U, Baroda.

Tennenbanm, Robert et al., 1959 : *Leadership and Organisation A Behavioural Science Approach*, New York, McGraw-Hills.

Taylor, Frederick, W., 1911 : *The Principles of Scientific Manament*. New York, Harper and Row.

Taylor, James and Bowers, David, G., 1972 : Survey of Organisations—A machine scored standardized Questionnaire Instrument : Ann Arbor, Michigan cited in Van de Ven A., and Ferry, D.L. (1980)

Turner, A.N. and Lawrence, Paul R., 1965 : *Industrial Jobs and the Worker : An Investigation of Response to Task Attributes Boston*, Mass : Harvard University Press.

Van de Ven, Andrew and Ferry, Daniel, L., 1980 : *Measuring and Assessing Organisations*, New York Wiley.

Veldsman, T.H. 1984 : Towards an Integrated View of the Concept Organisational Effectiveness. *Psychological Africana*, 21 : 63-77.

Vroom, V.H. 1964 : *Work and Motivation*, New York, John Wiley and Sons.

Vyasulu, P., 1984 : *Factors Related to Supervisory Performance in Manufacturing Units.* Indian Institute of Technology, Delhi, Ph. D. Thesis.

Weber, M., 1947 : *Theory of Social and Economic Organisations.* A.M. Henderson and T. Parsons. New York Free Press.

Weiner, Nan and Mahoney, Thomas, A., 1981 : A Model of Corporate Performance as a Function of Environmental Organisational and Leadership Influences. *Academy of Management Journal*, 24 : 453-471.

Wessel, C.J. et al., 1967 : *Criteria for Evaluating the Effectiveness of Library and Services.* John Thompson.

Wheeler Joseph L. and Goldhor Herbert, 1962 : *Practical Administration of Public Libraries*, New York, Harper and Row.

Wicker, A.W., 1968 : Undermanning Performance and Students Subjective Experiences in Setting of Small High Schools. *Journal of Personality and Social Psychology*, 10 : 255-261.

Wieker, A.W. and Mehler, A. 1971 : Assimilation of New Members in a Large and Small Church. *Journal of Applied Psychology*, 55 : 151-56.

Wolfe, J.N. et al. 1974 : *Economics of Technical Information System*, Preager Publishers.

Yutchman, E. and Seashore, S.E. 1967 : A System Resource Approach to Organisational Effectiveness. *American Sociological Review*, 32 : 891-903.

Index